AFRICAN ENTREPRENEURS
50 Success Stories

Iwa Adetunji

First edition published in 2017
© Copyright 2017
Iwa Adetunji

The right of Iwa Adetunji to be identified as the author of this work has been asserted by him in accordance with the Copyright, Designs and Patents Act 1998.

All rights reserved. No reproduction, copy or transmission of this publication may be made without express prior written permission. No paragraph of this publication may be reproduced, copied or transmitted except with express prior written permission or in accordance with the provisions of the Copyright Act 1956 (as amended). Any person who commits any unauthorised act in relation to this publication may be liable to criminal prosecution and civil claims for damage.

Although every effort has been made to ensure the accuracy of the information contained in this book, as of the date of publication, nothing herein should be construed as giving advice. The opinions expressed herein are those of the author and contributors and not of MX Publishing.

Hardcover ISBN 978-1-78705-090-7
Paperback ISBN 978-1-78705-091-4
ePub ISBN 978-1-78705-092-1
PDF ISBN 978-1-78705-093-8

Published in the UK by MX Publishing
335 Princess Park Manor, Royal Drive, London, N11 3GX
www.mxpublishing.com

Cover design by Brian Belanger

CONTENTS

Foreword	i
Introduction	iii
About this book	v
Who should read this book?	v
What readers will learn	v
Why I wrote this book	vi
Book structure & format	vi
Enjoy the journey	vi
1. Abisola Kola-Daisi	2
2. Addis Alemayehou	9
3. Agyin Solomon	16
4. Alpesh Patel	22
5. Angel Nkwaya, Ngyenzi 'Nunu' Mugyenyi & Janet Mugume	31
6. Askwar Hilonga	36
7. Aya & Mounaz Abdelraouf	42
8. Ayokanmi and Toluwani Binutu	49
9. Bernard Kiwia	56
10. Bethlehem Tilahun Alemu	64
11. Bioku Rahmon Jimoh	72
12. Bitebo Gogo	78
13. Carine-Zoe Umutoni	85
14. Caroline Wanjiku	90
15. Charles Cooper & Mlen-Too Wesley	98
16. Colin Thornton	105
17. Danson Muchemi	111
18. Donald Bambara	118
19. Doug Hoernle	124
20. Elie Kuame	131
21. Emeka Akano	138
22. Emo Rugene	146
23. Eric Kacou	152
24. Eric Kinoti	159
25. Eugenie Nyirambonigaba	165
26. Gloria Kamanzi Uwizera	173

27.	Isaiah Olatunde Oladeji	179
28.	Jacqueline Chavonne Goliath	185
29.	Jason Njoku	193
30.	Joselyne Umutoniwase	199
31.	Joseph van Appia	205
32.	Kamal Budhabhatti	211
33.	Kasope Ladipo-Ajai	217
34.	Kelvin Macharia Kuria	223
35.	Lilian Makoi	230
36.	Musty Ahmed	237
37.	Mwangi Kirubi	243
38.	Osine &Anesi Ikhianosime	249
39.	Patricia Jumi	254
40.	Paul Magnus Oviawe	261
41.	Sam Turyatunga	268
42.	Sangu Delle	275
43.	Sesinam Dagadu	284
44.	Siki Kigongo	290
45.	Taofick Okoya	296
46.	Tiguidanke Mounir Camara	304
47.	Wycliffe Waweru Maina	310
48.	Yohanis Gebreyesus Hailemariam	316
49.	Yvette Atieno Ondachi	323
50.	Zibusiso Mkhwanazi	330

This book is dedicated to
my lovely wife and wonderful daughters,
who are my inspirational and greatest teachers.

FOREWORD

Dream and steps to fulfil it

For a successful entrepreneur, passion comes before the money. Aspiring entrepreneurs should not allow thoughts about business to remain a dream, but go out and take the first step to fulfil that dream.

An entrepreneur is someone that is looking for freedom, has the confidence and someone that wants to do something for him or herself. To fulfil a dream, one has to take it one day at a time. The most important thing is to take the first step. That will show what the second step should be.

While the product and service offered must be of the highest quality, it must be affordable. A profit must be made, but do not exceed limits. There must be fair value for money. To be a successful entrepreneur one must also have a competitive advantage. To achieve this, one should look carefully at why people are prepared to buy a product or service and make adjustments if necessary.

Aspiring entrepreneurs should decide on what they want to do and achieve in life, and then make sure to become a master in what they want to do. Once a master, make sure there is a market for the product or service and be realistic about what can be achieved.

The vision and company strategy must be as simple as possible to communicate, so that everybody can understand it.

Remember that nothing in life begins 'big'. To make it big, one should keep to a dream. A dream should be written on a piece of paper to look at, and to remind you of it. Do not just sing about it in the shower, otherwise it will fade away. Entrepreneurs should dream big and not think that big things are not for them.

Hang on to a dream, even when there are setbacks. Research has shown that the well-known business leaders in the world have accomplished success by hanging on to a dream. Success takes time.

In the entrepreneurial world it is accepted that talent alone is not enough to be successful. More attributes are needed like faith, enthusiasm, initiative, focus, physical exercise, perseverance, an inquiring mind, character, relationships, responsibility and confidence.

Talent does not mean anything without that important first step to accomplish something. Success with the first step energises one to go on to the next.

Dr Chris van der Merwe*
Chief Executive Officer
Curro Holdings

*Dr Van der Merwe is a well-known educationalist and entrepreneur who started the successful Curro independent school group in 1998 with 28 learners in the vestry of a church in Durbanville, South Africa. The schools have now grown to nearly 50 in all provinces of South Africa.

INTRODUCTION

African Entrepreneurs 50 Success Stories is by no means a comprehensive story on the select African entrepreneurs. However, the basic premise is to give few pages synopsis of each of them and their chosen field of endeavours. It's a sort of snappy reference and useful guide.

It is already a fact worth repeating that there is an entrepreneurial boom taking place in Africa now. A steady rise of young businessmen and women who are building successful, fast growing companies in all fields of endeavours, and that is still growing exponentially. In fact, in many African countries today, it's quite easy to compile hundreds of such emerging and successful entrepreneurs.

It is particularly important for young Africans to meet, on the pages of this book, some of the positive role models in our midst; be inspired by the success stories of other African entrepreneurs who have overcome barriers to achieve success.

It is often said that if you produce something of value, you will reap a handsome return. Said in another way, some people make less money for doing certain things simply because many people can do similar things, whereas others make enormous money for rendering certain service or work simply because not too many people can do so in such a way as to impact or add value to much more people. This can be said of these select Africans in this book.

The most difficult thing is the decision to act. The rest is merely tenacity.

- Amelia Earhart, Aviator

ABOUT THIS BOOK

African Entrepreneurs, 50 Success Stories is a celebration of notable achievements of select Africans and how they have managed to excel in their chosen fields despite all odds. It is also to spur other Africans, especially the younger ones to have a steadfast focus on their goals and aspirations. Each profile showcase the entrepreneur, area of endeavour as well as an interview in a question and answer format to give readers a broader view with a photo to illustrate it.

WHO SHOULD READ THIS BOOK?

If you are a young or not so young aspiring entrepreneur or if you are already one facing what appears to be insurmountable business related challenges, this book is for you. It is as well good for Africans as it is for other races as the core-ingredients of successful entrepreneurs are universal.

WHAT READERS WILL LEARN

Whether you are young or old, in business or aspiring to get your feet wet, this book will not disappoint you. It will inspire you, it will enthral you and it will motivate you. You will not only read about success stories, but how these savvy men and women evolved to be effectively where they are now. It is essential to know that Africans, with even more daunting challenges and notwithstanding their background can overcome and surpass entrepreneur related issues. You will find that while some people are natural entrepreneurs, anyone can pursue entrepreneurship successfully if they put in what it takes. As Desiderius Erasmus, the Dutch Social Critic and Scholar once said, "Fortune favours the audacious." In short, the common denominator of all these entrepreneurs is - if you have a goal, you have to go for it and not wait for it to come to you.

WHY I WROTE THIS BOOK

In my 15 years as a media owner and executive, I have come in direct and indirect contact with many African success stories. Many are iconic and unsung. These African trailblazers are filling up big holes in the labour market by providing huge pool of jobs for others. This negates the narratives bounded around by some that Africans are mere consumers instead of creators and producers. It's therefore a fulfilment of a nagging feeling to highlight some of these men and women who are striving daily, using their business acumen to play pivotal roles in solving socio-economic problems for positive change.

BOOK STRUCTURE & FORMAT

It's written in a two-column format which makes it simple and readable. The first part on each entrepreneur has the photo, name and business, followed by a brief write-up about the entrepreneur and the business; concluding in a question and answer interview format. These diverse questions range from 15 to 20. Most of them include their favourite quote which is quite fascinating and says a lot about them. Sprinkled between each profile is an inspiring and thought provoking quote by past or present visionaries that relates well with the subject of this book.

ENJOY THE JOURNEY

Through the pages, you are going to meet incredible and visionary Africans both in Africa and in the diaspora, with inspiring stories that lend credence to the saying by Jesse Jackson, the African-American leader that, "If my eyes can see it, if my mind can conceive it, and my heart can believe it, I know I can achieve it."

The successful warrior is the average man, with laser-like focus.

- Bruce Lee, Martial Artist & Actor

AFRICAN ENTREPRENEURS
50 Success Stories

ABISOLA KOLA-DAISI
Florence H Boutique

Abisola Kola-Daisi is the Chief Executive Officer of Florence H Boutique, a luxury shoe and accessories store in Lagos, Nigeria. Her store is known to be the prime location in Lagos for some of the most sought after high-end fashion designers. She is also a Luxury Lifestyle Influencer across a digital platform through her online blog, AbiKD.com and through her social media presence. She curates content that evokes style, class, and culture through her travels across iconic cities.

The Interview:

How did the idea for your business come about?

The idea for Florence H Boutique stemmed from my penchant for luxurious and glamorous footwear and the women in Lagos who share the same love but have to wait to get on a plane to feed their insatiable appetites for beautiful shoes. This need brought forth the idea of an exclusive boutique to cater to the needs of the upbeat and fashion forward women of Nigeria and West Africa as a whole, located in their backyard. As for my blog, I like to share my experiences with an audience that will truly appreciate it. I am a visionary, and sometimes I feel the need to express my experiences publicly to my supporters via my online platforms.

Give the readers some insight into your business?

Florence H Boutique is an upscale women's boutique that opened in the highbrow area of Victoria Island in Lagos Nigeria in 2012. Florence H carries beautiful designer shoe labels for professional and sophisticated women. While our goal is to run a successful boutique, expansion plans include potentially franchising retail stores of the brands we carry, as we continue to penetrate a sizeable portion of the West African Market.

In your opinion, what do you consider as some of the top skills needed to be a successful entrepreneur?

I would say that having the right attitude is something that will go a long way in any business. I'm a very determined and strong-minded business woman. I know what I want, so I make sure to do the necessary work to achieve my goals. As a female entrepreneur, I have to be able to focus on my objectives and see them through any adversity I may endure. That is a big part of who I am in general, and I think if it weren't for that mentality, I wouldn't have achieved half of the things I'm doing now.

What demographic group would you consider as your key clients?

I would say that affluent, fashion-forward women in their 20's and 30's are the target. Though, as a creative, I don't feel the need to limit an audience. I create content that is direct reflection of my lifestyle, and I believe that if anyone is drawn to it, then by all means, I appreciate that support.

What have been some of your challenges and lessons learned from them?

I would say that one of the toughest challenges is overcoming public scrutiny. Since I am the daughter of a former Oyo State Governor, my life has been highly profiled in the public eye through the media. Public perception can sometimes be extremely critical of my choices, and thus my privacy can be invaded. I've had to learn to overcome that scrutiny and realise that I have goals to reach. If I spent my time worried or stressed about so much criticism, then I don't think that I could really get anything done. I think it's important to stay focused regardless of any distractions.

In today's challenging world, what do you do to stay on top of the game?

I would reiterate my position on maintaining a positive and strong attitude. That paired with some form of Faith can certainly help any individual stay grounded and focused on overall goals. Anything can be achieved as long as you have the right attitude.

What does success mean to you and the best way to achieve long-term success?

Success to me means a life full of joy and happiness; having enough faith in what I've done to know that my hard work was/is worth it and being at peace with that. To be successful is to reach a desired point where goals and aspirations you've set over the years are achieved. Having said that, my family is my main source of happiness and to know that I'm blessed with such love makes me feel successful regardless of whether set goals are met or not. Success is a constant growth. As we attain goals we set new ones. Therefore, success is an evolving desire. Whether it "goes" is dependent on the individual. If you view yourself as successful you're really the only one that can take that away from yourself."

What has been your most satisfying moment in business?

I think one of the most satisfying parts of my business is being able to have such a broad influence through the use of my digital platforms. We live in a digital age, and the way the World is connected now is insane. I have followers and supporters from all over the World, and I think that has been the most satisfying part of it all because there are people who care about the things that I like to share with them.

How has being an entrepreneur affected your (family) life?

Any entrepreneur can agree that running your own business can prove to be difficult while having a family. I'm a wife and mother, and the pressure can be very strong when trying to juggle everything at once. Thankfully, I can still be a busy woman and yet, my family and I manage to make it work as a unit.

What other sacrifices have you made to be a successful entrepreneur?

Generally, the biggest sacrifice is losing time. Not that time dedicated to my businesses is in vain, quite the opposite. But more so, I'd say that as an entrepreneur, you won't get the opportunity to go to every event or every milestone. I have friends in many cities that are absolutely dear to me, yet I don't get to see them often due to my work and family. It takes a lot of discipline to keep all of those things balanced.

On average, how many hours do you work per day and what is your typical day like?

It's hard to pinpoint exactly how many hours I work per day, as that varies each week. I have contacts in different time zones, so sometimes my work day is spread throughout various time frames from morning to night. An example would be spending my day checking proper inventory procedures for Florence H, then creating visual content in the afternoon for my blog, and finishing up in the evening with a conference call from my PR team in Los Angeles.

Where do you see yourself and business in another 10 years?

For Florence H, my goal is to continue to run a successful boutique with expansion plans of franchising retail stores of the brands we carry. With my public influence, I want to be able to serve as a global ambassador for female entrepreneurs and help them stay motivated in achieving their goals. My latest venture is a lifestyle brand that I'm calling AKD Brand, which will consist of luxury candles, home décor, and eventually an apparel line. It's currently in development stages, but I plan on it becoming a global luxury brand in the future.

What are your guiding personal and business principles?

Faith and discipline are the two most important factors for me as my business guides. If I feel within my spirit that I shouldn't go forward with any specific business deals, I don't do it. I've definitely made big decisions based on my own intuition, and my Faith and discipline certainly play a big factor in determining those things.

What is your best aspect of being an entrepreneur?

My best aspect is being a woman! Female entrepreneurs are being celebrated presently more than ever before in history. I get motivated every day when I see so many women around the world making power moves. It is such an amazing feeling to be a woman and to be able to run a business in such a competitive world.

Do you have role models and why?

My role models are my parents. They taught me to be a strong woman and to have a focused mind. Growing up, they demonstrated so much love and wisdom to me that I see that as a quality I can pass on to my own children.

What are your hobbies and what do you do to relax?

I absolutely love to travel. When I actually have time to do so, I make it a point to travel and experience so much that the world has to offer. I like to take in all of the sights from different places and then use those experiences to share with my supporters through my blog.

What advice or message do you have for young Africans who want to become entrepreneurs?

I think my advice would be geared more towards African women looking to start their own businesses, and what I would say to them is: Right now is the best time to be a female entrepreneur. The world is changing at a rapid pace, and there's still a long way to go before we see a true shift in gender equality in the workplace, but right now, it is so inspiring to see women of all walks coming into their businesses and beginning to dominate their industries. I want that to be their motivation and share that women can be excellent entrepreneurs. Women are serious forces to be reckoned with when it comes to business, and we deserve the same opportunities as men.

There is no easy walk to freedom anywhere, and many of us will have to pass through the valley of the shadow of death again and again before we reach the mountaintop of our desires.

- Nelson Mandela

ADDIS ALEMAYEHOU
251 Communications

Addis Alemayehou is the founder and Managing Partner of 251 Communications in Addis Ababa, Ethiopia. It is a PR/Communication firm with a clear goal of providing communication services for various private as well as public clients.

Alemayehou is also the founder of Paconet Media PLC, a privately held media firm. Paconet is the principal partner in the first privately held English FM Radio station (105.3 Afro FM) as well as other interests in Ethiopia. He is also co-founder of the newest Kana TV which is an Ethiopian general entertainment, free-to-air, satellite TV channel bringing international standard programming to the Ethiopian population. Alemayehou is equally engaged with Brand Africa, a pan-African inter-generational movement to create a positive image of Africa, celebrate Africa's identity and inspire competitiveness as a brand counsel.

Alemayehou who was awarded a Distinguished Service Award from the US Department of State serves on the Board of ICTET, the private sector ICT association in Ethiopia; on the Board of the Ethiopian American Business Forum, and on the Board of the African leadership network, the premier gatherings of the "Next" leaders of Africa who meet once a year to share ideas and promote inter Africa cooperation.

The Interview:

How did the idea for your business come about?

So much of marketing today falls flat and it misses the point - the point of sale where consumers engage and the buying decision gets made. So we are obsessed with unearthing insights and discovering new brand dimensions. Why? Because insight provides inspiration and inspiration is the springboard of all creativity.

Give us some insight into your business?

We are full-fledged communications and public relations firm with offices in the Washington, D.C. Metropolitan Area and Addis Ababa, Ethiopia. At 251 Communications, we manage our international and local clients'. We have partnerships with many of the leading service research and media agencies inside and outside of Ethiopia. At 251, we believe in innovative thinking; we work passionately taking a unique and creative approach to every project. Since 2010 we have delivered integrated solutions tailored to the specific needs of each client creating real and effective brand value. We have an open office concept that welcomes a family like atmosphere.

Since our inception, we have adopted a very hybrid working environment. There are practically no job titles (only there for you to identify us). Everyone works together to the culmination of each and every project!

In your opinion, what do you consider as some of the top skills needed to be a successful entrepreneur?

You have to be a risk taker and you should be able to find swift and precise solutions to problems. You ought to develop your inter-person and networking skills that helps while building relationships. I sincerely believe that being patient pays off.

What demographic group would you consider as your key clients?

Generally, 18 to 35-year old or the new millennia is our target demography but this will change depending on the type of product we are selling and the interest of our clients.

What have been some of your challenges and lessons learned from them?

Today, most of our target audience have access to all types of information and brands in a fraction of a second and more choices are available from across the globe. Before we didn't have this luxury and the dynamic was completely different. Growing up and until recent years we didn't have Facebook, YouTube, Twitter, LinkedIn, Instagram etc... therefore in comparison that period of time was by far easier to manage our types of businesses. To cope with the change we have adapted to the current market needs and have customised our approaches accordingly.

In today's challenging world, what do you do to stay on top of the game?

My team and I have made it our priority to be well informed and ahead at all times; our type of business rewards sharpness and speed. I am usually up before everybody and go to sleep after everyone else.

What does success mean to you and the best way to achieve long-term success?

Success is doing what you love and making a living out of it rather than doing what someone else wants you do to. The best way to achieve long term success is to always innovate, understand the market needs and make a calculated forecast of the future market needs as well.

What has been your most satisfying moment in business?

Co-launching Afro FM 105.3 radio station and Kana TV station with my partners.

How has being an entrepreneur affected your (family) life?

My wife and family are supportive and understand the dynamics of our business but it does not change the fact that I spend a lot of my time at work with different work related engagements and that has taken time away from my family.

What other sacrifices have you made to be a successful entrepreneur?

As I mentioned earlier I missed out on time that I would have loved to spend with my family, missed out on holidays. Basically I have differed satisfaction in order to build these businesses.

On average, how many hours do you work per day and what is your typical day like?

13 - 14 hours a day is dedicated to my work. I am up at 6:00 a.m. and meet clients for breakfast at 7:30 a.m. which is mostly the first meeting of the day. I get to the office by 8:30 a.m. and start my daily routine - check my emails and related issue until 10:00 a.m., followed by meetings with various clients till 12 noon. I would like to reiterate that I value these regular meetings because I believe that they are

opportunities that help me understand the background, business philosophy and needs of each client. Around mid-day I go to the gym and the afternoon is mostly geared towards strategy meeting, overseeing events which could also take place in the mornings depending on the programme.

Where do you see yourself and business in another 10 years?

I see my businesses flourishing and growing in capacity and quality. I plan to take these businesses and new business ideas to at least 20 African countries and to oversee 10-15 companies in different sectors.

What are your guiding personal and business principles?

Don't do anything that you don't want done to you.

What is your greatest fear, and how do you manage fear?

I fear not being able to spend time as much as I want to with my family. I try to manage it by creating quality time for the times that we have.

What is your best aspect of being an entrepreneur?

Someone that sees opportunity where others see problems and someone that is willing to risk it all to execute his idea.

Do you have role models and why?

Yes, I do have role models in different areas of my life; my father for his love for Africa, Ethiopia. As a parent both my parents are my role models as they groomed me to be a better person. My sister, for always "keeping it real". In the business world as well, I have role models that changed and influenced my line of thoughts... I don't know everything therefore I seek inspirations from great minds.

What are your hobbies and what do you do to relax?

Given the time that I allocate for socialising, I am a person that loves spending time with family and friends and reading books.

Do you have any favourite quote or saying?

Just do it - Nike

What advice or message do you have for young Africans who want to become entrepreneurs?

There is no better time than now to venture into your own business; think, plan and execute.

Whatever you want in life, other people are going to want too. Believe in yourself enough to accept the idea that you have an equal right to it.

- Diane Sawyer, Journalist

AGYIN SOLOMON
King Solomon Trading

Agyin Solomon is the founder and Managing Director of King Solomon Trading in Antwerp, Belgium.

King Solomon Trading is a bulk food and non-food brokers selling to grocery wholesalers, independent retailers and food service distributors in the Belgium and other European countries. In addition, it operates its own well-stocked stores in Belgium.

In business since 1995, King Solomon Trading is one of the most renown and successful Cash and Carry food warehouse in Europe.

The Interview:

How did the idea for your business come about?

As a secondary school drop-out in Ghana, I left for Nigeria for a 'greener pasture'. I started out there as a shopkeeper, but after gaining some experience, I returned to Ghana to start my own business. I would go to Nigeria to purchase auto spare parts and electrical materials which I sold in Ghana. Likewise, in Ghana, I would buy vinyl plywood and other related materials to sell in Nigeria. The military coup of 1985 destabilised my business and so, I decided to travel to Europe. I worked odd jobs in Belgium for about 5 years before starting out on my own. My first venture was buying shoes, bags and clothes from Italy to sell in Belgium. At the beginning, I would hawk my wares on the streets and in café bars in the city, but I later opened a shop to sell these items. However, it soon dawned on me that it would be more profitable to start selling tropical foods and cosmetics to my fellow Africans as there was no such shop then. That was how it all started.

In your opinion, what do you consider as some of the top skills needed to be a successful entrepreneur?

In my type of business, you do not require a diploma or a university degree to make it a success. Most importantly, you need to be very creative and disciplined. For example, I did not have the relevant document to start a business in Europe, but knowing what I wanted, I got the help of someone else and after a while, I took over completely. You need to know what you want, work towards it and be prepared to learn from your mistakes as you go along. Tenacity is important.

What demographic group would you consider as your key clients?

Both on the retail and wholesale levels, 80 percent of our clients are fellow Africans while the rest are Asians and others who have need for our products.

What have been some of your challenges and lessons learned from them?

At the beginning, it was the police raids. They would patrol near my store to question and ask for identification cards of all Africans in sight. It happened quite often and as result, some were even deported back to Africa. I had to personally protest to the Mayor and the Police Chief in the city to stop the harassment. I was arrested and locked up. The news was in both Belgium and the Netherlands' television stations. Eventually I wrote a petition to the Commissioner of Police who instructed that I be left alone, since I was paying my taxes. Nowadays, things have improved, except of-course the huge taxes that come with running a big business in Belgium.

Regarding lessons learned, the food inspectors have made the business more focussed on providing quality food from Africa. You cannot but be on your toes and be alert with what you import into Europe, knowing that a small mistake can cost you a lot in penalty fees as well as lost revenue from the confiscation or destruction of improper food items.

In today's challenging world, what do you do to stay on top of the game?

The only way is to keep learning from errors and mistakes and to try and get better and better.

What does success mean to you and the best way to achieve long-term success?

With what I do, I have been able to accomplish a lot for myself, my family and my community. It's a good feeling. For a long-term success, it's important to be committed and be honest to everyone you deal with.

What has been your most satisfying moment in business?

There are several. As a result of my business, I now get recognition from people; even long lost friends seek out for me.

How has being an entrepreneur affected your (family) life?

Due to the demand of the business, it's quite easy to lose your family. At the beginning, my wife and I were both working 16-hours per day with our children spending a lot of time with the Nanny.

What other sacrifices have you made to be a successful entrepreneur?

Losing quality time with family is the biggest. I have been very luck though. I'm a father of six children with three of them currently in the university.

On average, how many hours do you work per day and what is your typical day like?

At the beginning, I could only manage 3 to 4 hours sleep a night. However, I still work 14 to 15 hours a day on average.

Where do you see yourself and business in another 10 years?

At my age, it's doubtful that I can continue to work as I do now in 10 years. I hope to get the business to the level that it would be much easier for my children or anyone who would be running it then.

What are your guiding personal and business principles?

I respect the rights of my clients and do not impose my wills on them. Likewise, I do not show any superiority to people either in personal or business level. I'm jovial and friendly to all.

What is your greatest fear, and how do you manage fear?

With my experience, business accountants in Europe are by far my biggest headache as I have had to change them three or four times during the course of my business. If care is not taken, they can destroy overnight what you have worked for all your life. It seems they work for the government and not for you. As a safeguard, I have asked some of my children to study accounting and economics in school to protect themselves against my bad experiences with accountants.

What is your best aspect of being an entrepreneur?

Being independent is always good because it brings great benefit. For those who do not derive benefit or satisfaction, it may not be for them.

Do you have role models and why?

Yes, my role model was the great entrepreneur, late MKO Abiola of Nigeria. While in Nigeria, I saw how he worked hard and gave a lot to charity. Another was late Appenteng Mensah of Ghana who had salt industry and several other trade businesses.

What are your hobbies and what do you do to relax?

I love football very much. I used to play for NEPA football team in Nigeria and I'm now the founder and owner of a top division football team in Ghana.

What advice or message do you have for young Africans who want to become entrepreneurs?

My message would be to young Africans in Europe. Although, there are lots of challenges, but there are also lots of opportunities for those who are prepared to take the bull by the horn. For instance, Asians are in the majority when it comes to selling our own food and products to us. What's stopping us from doing the same? There should be more of us in the wholesale food business in Europe than what currently obtain. We should not only be satisfied with doing odd jobs for ever, but seek to explore legitimate challenges that would make us independent.

We all have ability; the difference is how we use it.

-      Stevie Wonder, Singer & Songwriter

ALPESH PATEL
mi-Fone

Alpesh Patel is the founder and Chief Executive Officer of mi-Fone, the first African Mobile Devices brand which started in 2008; probably one of the first tech start-ups on the African continent. He literally built the business from nothing as there was no funding for seven years and so it was a completely bootstrapped Pan African operation.

Patel's team members have worked with various companies such as Motorola, Coca-Cola, RazorFish, Microsoft, Deloitte, and Phillips, with a team presence spanning over 5 countries.

mi-Fone is designed in Africa and made in China using superior components and technology on par with other well-known international brands. It currently has a footprint in over 15 countries throughout Africa, with plans to rapidly continue to grow over the next five years.

The Interview:

How did the idea for your business come about?

The idea came about for having been with Motorola for many years and understanding that the big brands do some good things but also miss out on a lot of things. We figure out that African things are best done by Africans themselves and that the mass market is actually missing out on what we call choice; reason why we developed a number of handsets with prices ranging from $5 to $50. For instance, I believe that the taxi driver in Nairobi, Kenya has different mobile needs than a 16-year-old school girl in Lagos.

Give the readers some insight into your business?

The business has been very difficult and I do speak a lot about the dark side of entrepreneurship and especially in Africa. I cannot speak for the highly sophisticated entrepreneurs in markets like the U.S. and Europe; I can only speak for myself as an entrepreneur for many years in Africa.

In your opinion, what do you consider as some of the top skills needed to be a successful entrepreneur?

I think one of the top skills required is to have a very thick skin because you are going to get the door shut in your face a lot and you are going to get people who just don't want to talk to you because you are a small business. You have got to be very resilient. I think resilience is the key as one has to get up from mistakes and failures and not really take no for answer

What demographic group would you consider as your key clients?

Key clients are the African youth in terms of branding. If you look at mi-Fone, you will see that we are the hip hop brand in the telecom industry, and for us it would always be about the emotional attachment to the brand. We are not about moving boxes but about moving values.

What have been some of your challenges and lessons learned from them?

Some of the biggest challenges are the lack of empowerment for the entrepreneurs. Entrepreneurs here are not fast or flourishing enough like in bigger economies, where they are favoured and looked upon as the engine of innovation, whereas in Africa, the big boys tend to buy from the big boys. One of the lessons I've really learned from my experience is not to get the business at any cost. For instance, we have never paid any bribes and handed out brown envelopes (which would probably have made us more successful) but then where is our integrity? I always run the business in a very ethical manner. We have been a David running against many Goliaths. The only thing we have going is the innovation and creativity.

In today's challenging world, what do you do to stay on top of the game?

That is very subjective because I don't think I'm on top of the game because we are not even in the top five in terms of the African market share, but I believe we are very good at surviving because we have gone through a lot and it's been a tough journey but we manage to build this business with no money and that by itself means that we can showcase our story. It means that even in Africa, you can run ethical business with full disclosure without big funding

What does success mean to you and the best way to achieve long-term success?

Success to me means surviving against all the odds. Success is definitely subjective, although a cliché that success is a journey and not a destination, and I think the best way to achieve long term success is to continue doing what you are doing, continue solving problems and adding value. If we continue to solve problems that exist in Africa today, I think success will come. If we can continue serving and solving problems of the target market and providing customers with cool innovative offerings products to help them perform better, I think we would have made our little contributions.

What has been your most satisfying moment in business?

Most satisfying moment in my business is just basically building this. It's been really tough but just getting a lot of mileage out of this and getting the brand out there and that people know about us. To be able to build something out of nothing is to me a success. The Most satisfying is building something that belongs to us, and I mean us Africans

How has being an entrepreneur affected your (family) life?

Yes, being an entrepreneur does affect your family life. Luckily for me, I was already on the move, even before I started mi-Fone. My wife is used to my travels and being on the road a lot. However, my tip to any entrepreneur is that you have got to get your family to support you 100%; otherwise you are going to have a really tough time because you don't see them, and if you are not in front of your clients, how do you succeed? It doesn't matter if you are a tech entrepreneur, scientific or otherwise, if you are not selling your game, you can have the best technology, but if no one knows nothing about it, it's not going to work. Yes, I have made a lot of sacrifices and have forgone many holidays, even the first two years; I didn't earn any salary and had lots of challenges in terms of cash flow. Customers pay you late and that's often the African way of doing things, and they pay you last because you are one of their smallest suppliers and they may want to take their chances. I have had to deal with irregular cash flows and that means the challenges of not being able to pay your bills on time, pay your rents on time. These are some of the sacrifices you have to make.

On average, how many hours do you work per day and what is your typical day like?

Typical day would be 12 to 15 hours with a combination of early morning exercise. I'm part of the 5 a.m. initiative introduced by my good friend Robin Sharma. I believe in going for walks as that makes one think better. I believe in not spending excessive time in front of the computer and I believe in having productive meetings. I could fill my whole day with meetings but it won't get you anywhere unless there is a purpose behind it. My meetings also don't last more than 30 minutes.

What are your guiding personal and business principles?

One of the principles that I have is that I just don't give any credit and people just abuse your goodwill. My business principles are quite different now than when I first started and I think that's a test of what I and my business have gone through. There are lots of principles that I live or work with. I tend to keep a very tight circle of network. You have to be very careful of those you talk to about your ideas. Another thing is also I started off as very emotional but in the business world I found out that being emotional does not always help and you learn to keep some emotions in check as outsiders can see it as a weakness and abuse the faith you put in them. Not everyone out there has good intentions!

What is your greatest fear, and how do you manage fear?

Just starting Mi-Fone was fearful but I managed to do it, so fear for me is when you live inside your comfort zone and I have always lived outside of my comfort zone. Fear is something we all have - it's how we look at it - as an opportunity to grow or to remain in the same place. The best way I feel to manage fear is to just do it. Do the thing that you fear most and it all starts falling into place.

What is your best aspect of being an entrepreneur?

I do not consider myself a good leader. I think I'm a leader without a title. I get a lot of my inspiration from the teachings and writings from one of my friends and mentor, Robert Sharma, one of the top 5 Leadership Experts on the planet… It's about trying to be one of the best that you can be and not try to change for anyone else. Why change when you are born to standout. Since I have been a kid, I have always been a rebel with a cause and not a rebel without a cause. There's always been this call inside me to go up against the status quo and just challenge the status quo. I think being a "true" self starter Entrepreneur is my best aspect; the fact that I believe something is possible out of nothing

Do you have role models and why?

Robert Sharma is definitely my role model because of his teachings. Baraka Obama is another and I look up to the Hip Hop moguls like Dr Dre, 50 cent, Puffy, Jay Z etc as they have built empires out of nothing. They don't come from cushy backgrounds but they overcame the odds and made it. Their story is my story and I can relate to that much better than I can with other well known folks

What are your hobbies and what do you do to relax?

Regular exercise, reading, listening to my RnB, Hip Hop, House music and good food. I have a modus operandi on how I work; it's called PESHMODE and my work now involves Public speaking and advising others on what pitfalls to look out for on their entrepreneur journeys.

Do you have any favourite quote or saying?

I have quite a few and some of them are:
"You are not a real hustler unless you lose it all… and get it all back.";
"If you don't have your own skin in the game, you will never have accountability… once you have your own money on the table, you are just more careful. So if you are going to start your own business, put your own money down."
"When someone tells me 'No', it doesn't mean I can't do it; it simply means I can't do it with them."

"I'd rather have the mo'money problems than the no'money problem".

"Knowing that you've made the same mistake twice is called having 'experience'.

What advice or message do you have for young Africans who want to become entrepreneurs?

My advice to young aspiring African entrepreneurs is that I don't really wish entrepreneurship on anyone because I think it's a very tough game. You have to be really ready for it and I think it's one of those things that really sound very glamorous. When you think about it, 30 years ago, our parents wanted us to be doctors and lawyers and I never listened to my parents, and 15 years ago, everyone wanted to be Investment bankers and today everyone wants to be entrepreneurs. The difference between an entrepreneur and the first two is that in good and bad times, a doctor and a lawyer will make money. Likewise, in good and bad times, if Investment bankers fail, someone will bail them out. As entrepreneur, especially in Africa, you are on your own. There's no support system as you cannot go to a family or friend, and so you cannot pay your bills and have sleepless nights, worrying where your next meal will come from. Entrepreneurship, especially in Africa is not for the faint hearted. If your will is not there, don't even think about it. There's nothing wrong with a pay check, there's nothing wrong with 9-5 work, there's nothing wrong with spending the weekend and holidays with your children and family. It's always been my dream right from a young age that if I have to spend 70-80-90 years in this planet, I want to do whatever I can to make something out of my life and if I have to run around, I might as well run around for myself rather than for other people and build a brand that belongs to us and more so the experience that I have had in my life, I think I would have made a bigger difference in other people's lives than if I would be working in a corporate environment of 9-5. Who I am today is the combination of who I am, my mistakes and my experiences in life. So, if you are ready for such journey, make the types of mistakes that I have made, then go ahead, but don't even think about starting a business if you are not solving a problem and if you don't have some funding. Let your ego go - there is nothing wrong with being someone's No.2 - at least the headaches will be secondary.

When you're that successful, things have a momentum, and at a certain point you can't really tell whether you have created the momentum or it's creating you.

- Annie Lennox, singer and songwriter

ANGEL NKWAYA, NGYENZI 'NUNU' MUGYENYI & JANET MUGUME
Bold Kampala

The idea and concept of the Bold Kampala in Uganda was conceived by the trio of Angel Nkwaya, Ngyenzi 'Nunu' Mugyenyi and Janet Mugume.

Angel Nkwaya has training in Human Resource Management (BA), Project Management and Public Relations. She has years of experience in retail management, including the position of Store Manager at Jenni Button, a member of the Platinum Group in Cape Town, South Africa.

Ngyenzi 'Nunu' Mugyenyi is an entrepreneur in the fashion industry, with an MPS in Fashion Merchandising and Retails Management, as well as training in Interior Decor. She also has years of experience in the retail industry, both in Africa and the US, most recently in the marketing department at Authentic Brands Group in New York.

Janet Mugume has training in Property Studies (B.Sc), Real Estate & Property Investments (M.Sc) and Marketing & Advertising. She spent couple of years as the Client Service Account Executive at Ogilvy in Kampala, Uganda.

These women entrepreneurs have a vision for raising

awareness of, and retailing through their African fashion brands. BOLD Kampala retail concept provides affordable space and excellent exposure for uniquely African designer fashion brands both locally and internationally.

The award winning BOLD Kampala has over thirty clothing and accessory brands from six different African countries.

The Interview:

How did the idea for your business come about?

On our return to Uganda, we quickly identified two problem areas. One, there was nowhere convenient to purchase affordable clothing. Two, there was nowhere affordable for designers to open up convenient outlets. With minimal savings and a huge leap of faith, we opened BOLD Kampala

Give the readers some insight into your business?

Founded June 1st 2012, Bold Kampala is an award-winning, Ugandan-based, retail outlet that houses over 30 up-and-coming designers from countries across the African continent including Uganda, Kenya, Rwanda, Burundi, Nigeria, Ghana, Tunisia and South Africa.

In your opinion, what do you consider as some of the top skills needed to be a successful entrepreneur?

An entrepreneurial spirit: ambition, fearlessness

Self-discipline: Working for yourself means you're accountable to yourself. Set goals and see to it that you meet them.

Resilience: starting your business can be very challenging. You will need to overcome challenges - over and over again.

Humility: Learn not only from your mistakes but from the mistakes of others.

What demographic group would you consider as your key clients?

Women between the ages of 25 and 45. We carry a variety of designers, each with different styles that collectively cater to a wide variety of women.

What have been some of your challenges and lessons learned from them?

As the first of our kind in the region, there were several barriers to break. We still continue breaking barriers today.

While we have had to learn from our mistakes, we have also had the opportunity to learn valuable lessons from successful business men and women our entrepreneurial journey. We remain grateful for their mentorship.

Perhaps the greatest challenge has been falling down and getting back up. Over and over again. This continues to be a learning experience for us.

In today's challenging world, what do you do to stay on top of the game?

We don't stand still. We don't get comfortable. We are constantly looking for ways to move forward.

What does success mean to you and the best way to achieve long-term success?

Growth. We have set goals and targets for ourselves - long and short term. For us, success is achieving them. As we continue to work towards these targets, we regularly re-visit them as a reminder to stay focused on making them come to life.

What has been your most satisfying moment in business?

We have celebrated a few milestones over the last four years including a world tour, and this year, the opening of a second store in Kigali, Rwanda.

How has being an entrepreneur affected your (family) life?

We come from an entrepreneurial background and remain grateful for the guidance and support that we have received from family and friends that are on entrepreneurial journeys of their own.

On average, how many hours do you work per day and what is your typical day like?

Our days vary, depending on what projects we are working on. Some days we have had to work through the night, and others only require a few hours. There is no such thing as a day-off for us.

Where do you see yourself and business in another 10 years?

Bigger. Better. Bolder.

What is your greatest fear, and how do you manage fear?

Failure. Fear is crippling. In order to overcome this, we have had to learn that it is okay to fail. Risk-taking is very much a part of the process, at the very worst, we learn a lesson.

What is your best aspect of being an entrepreneur?

Watching an idea come to life is most satisfying. It comes with a huge sense of accomplishment, independence and confidence. We are our own bosses.

What advice or message do you have for young Africans who want to become entrepreneurs?

Do something you're good at. Choose your business partners wisely. Give it everything you've got. Don't give up.

No man who continues to add something to the material, intellectual and moral well-being of the place in which he lives is long left without proper reward.

- Booker T. Washington, Educator, Writer and Orator

ASKWAR HILONGA
Nanofilter

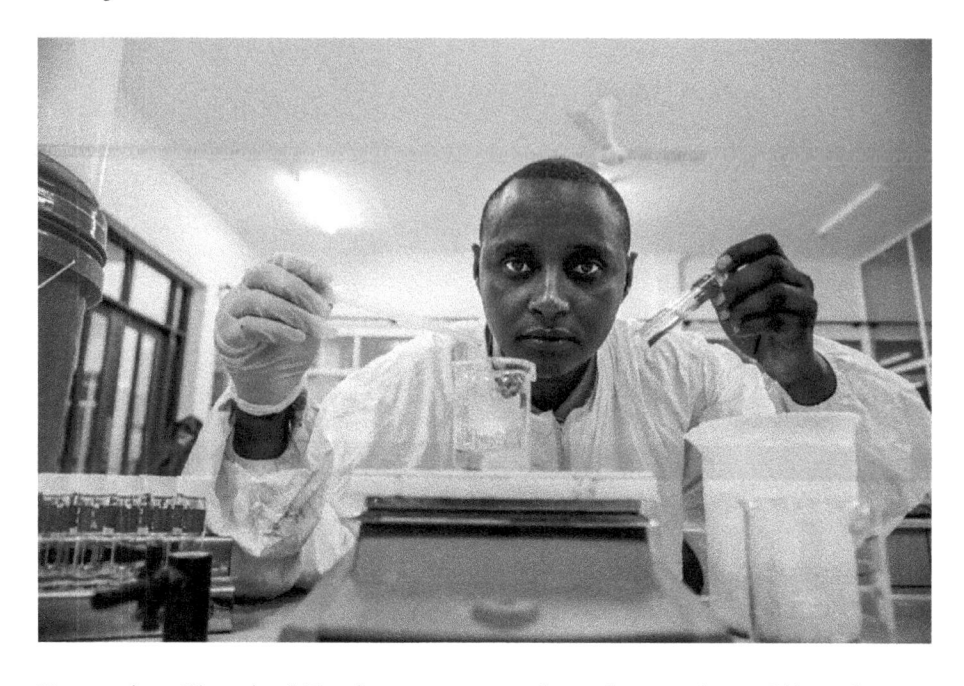

Tanzanian Chemical Engineer Dr. Askwar Hilonga is the inventor of Nanofilter, a low-cost customisable water filtration system that uses nanotechnology and sand to clean water. The filter traps all contaminants such as copper, fluoride, bacteria, viruses and pesticides from water to make it drinkable.

His ingenious invention is capable of transforming lives of many rural African communities to have access to safe drinking water and to reduce the number of lives lost to waterborne diseases.

His patented filtration system combines a slow sand filter with a combination of nanomaterials made from sodium silicate and silver to eliminate toxic heavy metals. Water first passes through the sand and then through the nanomaterials. Current water filtration units on the market offer a "one-size-fits–all" solution, whereas Nanofilter can target and eliminate contaminants that are specific to a particular geographic region.

Dr. Hilonga who is also a Senior Lecturer at The Nelson Mandela African Institution of Science and Technology, Tanzania, has received several awards, including Africa Prize for Engineering Innovation by the Royal Academy of Engineering, Pitch@Palace Africa by the Duke of York, Prince Andrew among many.

The Interview:

How did the idea for your business come about?

One, I saw a social need since my childhood. I grew up in a very poor family - suffering from water-borne diseases; two, technical capacity - I did my PhD in Nanomaterials that are suitable for water purification, among many other applications; three, business - I saw the market opportunity for water filters in Tanzania.

Give the readers some insight into your business?

At present we are focused on establishing and running WATER STATIONS operated by the Local Entrepreneurs. This project is now funded by the UK Government at GBP 35,000 for three years. The detailed business model is available on our website www.gongalimodel.com..

In your opinion, what do you consider as some of the top skills needed to be a successful entrepreneur?

Inter and Intra personal communication, commitment, hard work, connection, action action action!

What demographic group would you consider as your key clients?

For the water stations my main customers are the Local entrepreneurs, particularly in underserved communities. For direct sales of water filters my main customers are middle incomers.

What have been some of your challenges and lessons learned from them?

Recruiting the right people to work with has been a nightmare. My company is still at infant stage - so it is hard to get top-notch talented people because I cannot pay them satisfactorily. I therefore depend on fresh university graduates who are not stable - they leave at any time, whenever they see another greener pasture.

In today's challenging world, what do you do to stay on top of the game?

I am innovative on daily basis. There is no formula. What works today may not work tomorrow. So I am always on my toes - making decisions constantly/innovatively - every single day!

What does success mean to you and the best way to achieve long-term success?

To me success means impacting millions of lives! I want to be a millionaire of impacting millions of lives!

What has been your most satisfying moment in business?

That is when my product won the Africa Prize for Engineering Innovation, sponsored by The Royal Academy of Engineering, UK. This gave me a "Global Publicity", Global Network, Global attention, Enormous Media coverage, Grants up to GBP 350,000, Reputation, etc. WHAT ELSE DO I WANT ON EARTH?

How has being an entrepreneur affected your (family) life?

Unless my wife was the CEO of our company my marriage would have been broken! Even now it should be time for my family but I am using it for this interview - just imagine how my family feels! But my wife understands my circumstances and she bears with me. My kids are also learning step by step. I normally bring some gifts for them and take them for outing on weekends to compensate the time they missed me.

What other sacrifices have you made to be a successful entrepreneur?

I had to sleep at 10 pm and wake-up at 3 am almost every day, except on Sabbath day/Saturday. I gave-up many leisure so I can have more time to meet my objectives - some of them controversial.

On average, how many hours do you work per day and what is your typical day like?

As explained above. In addition, I have no time for stories when I get to the work place. If you find me chatting with someone then it must be something related or close to my business

Where do you see yourself and business in another 10 years?

I will be a millionaire in terms of money and in terms of millions of lives that I must have impacted.

What are your guiding personal and business principles?

To be innovative, to work hard, be focused, and LOVE PEOPLE AND GOD!

What is your greatest fear, and how do you manage fear?

I strongly believe in God. So most of the times I just pray if something bad is heading my way. I don't fear but hate poverty, sickness, and ignorance.

What is your best aspect of being an entrepreneur?

I am very very very committed, INNOVATIVE, and love God and humanity.

Do you have role models and why?

Nelson Mandela and Julius K. Nyerere. Those are very genuine, patriotic, and committed people - They truly wanted to give back to their communities/countries. I want to follow their footsteps for everything good they did.

What are your hobbies and what do you do to relax?

I like and play football, listen and sing Christian songs, play piano, read the Bible and other spiritual books, and enjoy "anything" with my family.

Do you have any favourite quote or saying?

"I can do all things through Him who gives me strength" Philipians 4:13. "He who has received a privilege of being educated is like a person in a starving village who is given a remaining supplies of food so he can have enough energy to bring supplies from a distant country. If he does not come back to serve his brothers and sisters he is a TRAITOR" - by Julius K. Nyerere. "Education is the great engine of human development. It is through education that a daughter of a peasant may become a doctor, a son of the miner becomes the mine owner, and the son of a farmer becomes the president of a great nation" - Nelson Mandela.

What advice or message do you have for young Africans who want to become entrepreneurs?

Don't look for jobs - look for your passion. If you work for your passion you will get everything you desire on earth... but Think BIG, Start small, Learn fast, Grow Quick!

Don't loaf and invite inspiration; light out after it with a club, and if you don't get it you will nonetheless get something that looks remarkably like it.

- Jack London, writer and social activist

AYA & MOUNAZ ABDELRAOUF
Okhtein

Egyptian design duo siblings Aya and Mounaz Abdelraouf launched their brand Okhtein - meaning, appropriately, "sisters" in Arabic - because of their vision to bring true luxury back to their home country as well as drawing international attention to the inherent refinement of Egyptian artisanship, sensing a gap in the market for true luxury accessories produced in Egypt.

Okhtein seeks to set new trends, promoting Egyptian artistry as well as presenting new designs to the world. As a brand, Okhtein is remarkable due to its hyper-local manufacturing process. Each product has a unique provenance with deep cultural associations.

To manufacture their products, Aya and Mounaz felt compelled to take a philanthropic approach to their work out of a desire to incorporate more handmade embroidery and straw into their leatherwork. This led to a highly mutually rewarding collaboration with several local NGOs that work to provide assistance to skilled female workers who have faced considerable financial hardship.

Okhtein stands apart as a luxury brand that is truly committed to supporting the cultural value of Egyptian craftsmanship and to giving back to those in need while promoting innovative, cutting-edge design on an international scale.

The Interview:

How did the idea for your business come about?

Both of us knew we would start working together after graduation. We shared the same interests in art, fashion and design. Mounaz graduated in 2012 with a degree in integrated marketing communications. She worked in J. Walter Thompson advertising company in Cairo for about a year. Aya also graduated from the same institution in 2013, but with a degree in communication and media arts. As soon as she graduated she started planning and researching the leather business in Egypt. After the market research, it took a year to launch our first collection.

Give the readers some insight into your business?

Our business is primarily focused on leather craftsmanship and artistry in Egypt. We create handbags and scarves made out of the finest materials in Cairo. We focus on a hyper local manufacturing process because we believe that's what sets us apart from other competing brands. We try to represent Egyptian artistry on a broader level, in addition to placing the country on the global fashion market.

In your opinion, what do you consider as some of the top skills needed to be a successful entrepreneur?

Having a positive mind is the key to becoming a successful entrepreneur. There are a lot of failed business opportunities because people don't believe in themselves. It is very important to be resilient because nothing comes easy and nothing good lasts forever. With good problem solving skills, determination and a positive mind- surely nothing is impossible. It is also key to know all your market gaps and needs and from there you cater a service.

What demographic group would you consider as your key clients?

We target upper and upper middle class women between the ages of 18-40. They are the hardworking women that support themselves. They want to buy their clothes, accessories and anything else they need on their own. They are our key clients because we offer trending bags that have superb quality but at the same time affordable when compared to big fashion labels.

What have been some of your challenges and lessons learned from them?

Some of the major lessons learned from the demographic group we are targeting is that they're always on the go. Their daily lives are extremely busy with constant new interests. As a brand, we need to keep up with this changing world of theirs in order to remain on top and in order to stay "hip".

In today's challenging world, what do you do to stay on top of the game?

We stay on top of the game by always being updated about what's around us. To understand fashion and trends you need to communicate with people outside your circle. Social media for example is our biggest tool. We feed our brains with so much information all under one platform. With new trends around us every single day, our job is study them well and change them around in order to present something new.

What does success mean to you and the best way to achieve long-term success?

Success to us is achieving our vision. When we started Okhtein we were very motivated because we had envisioned how the brand would look like now. Every phase we enter we sort of pre-planned it in our heads. To achieve long-term success it is important to always stay focused and motivated.

What has been your most satisfying moment in business?

When actress Emma Watson wore our bag without the help of any PR. Another satisfying moment in business and in our opinion might be our biggest achievement so far was when we raised our capital without seeking help from investors. We started off with 2,000 USD and managed to work around it to turn it into a big, and profitable business. Against all odds, we managed to use the sum we've had and turn it into a capital.

How has being an entrepreneur affected your (family) life?

It has affected our family in a positive way. Since we are family members working together it grew us closer and stronger. We trust each other blindly and that sets a promising work atmosphere and environment.

What other sacrifices have you made to be a successful entrepreneur?

To become a successful entrepreneur you need to realise that working hours are no longer from 9-5. You know own your business and as cliché as it sounds, it becomes your child. When you have a child you don't have specific hours a day where you watch over them. This applies to becoming a successful entrepreneur as well. You end up sacrificing free time, personal life and the time in general to do anything else but think of work.

On average, how many hours do you work per day and what is your typical day like?

We work around 12 hours a day on average. We try to maintain the 8 hour limit but it's very difficult because most of the time we end up discussing work related topics after hours and on weekends. Our typical day starts at our office at 10:30 am. Our workshop and office are in the same building, so we are in between both places up until 8pm when the workshop closes. Some days we run several errands outside the office, for example, visiting our supplier's workshops to ensure our quality.

Where do you see yourself and business in another 10 years?

We are hoping to expand our brand throughout the Middle East and to the world. We aspire to become an international accessory/fashion brand that is globally acknowledged and respected.

What are your guiding personal and business principles?

Integrity and fairness are our key principles for our personal and business lives.

What is your greatest fear, and how do you manage fear?

I wouldn't want to say failure because failure leads to success; you only learn through the hard times. Our biggest fear is losing the will power. That is the only constant you will have throughout any business endeavour. Numbers that determine success can change and it's the willpower that must stay consistent to go through any obstacle and fear.

What is your best aspect of being an entrepreneur?

The best aspect of being an entrepreneur is the independence that comes with it. You become your own boss and therefore, you end up pushing yourself to learn new things everyday in order to understand the business as a whole. You no longer depend on anyone to finish your work, so you explore new fields out of your comfort zone.

Do you have role models and why?

Anyone could be a role model. We can't pick one out because there's just so much around the world, both famous and unknown. We wouldn't be giving justice to all the women and all the men who live in small villages every day, fighting a battle we don't know of. That's why we believe that our perfect role model is any person who was able to achieve so much with so little, going against all odds.

What are your hobbies and what do you do to relax?

Our hobbies include working out to relieve stress, cooking, listening to music and reading. Listening to music helps us relax after long stressful days.

Do you have any favourite quote or saying?

"If you are working on something exciting that you really care about, you don't have to be pushed. The vision pulls you"- Steve Jobs.

What advice or message do you have for young Africans who want to become entrepreneurs?

Nothing is impossible. If you really want something so bad, you need to work for it and before you work for it, you need to envision it. You need to believe in the good part of life, the part that drives you to speak up and show who you truly are. Do good, have faith in what you want to accomplish and rest assured anything you want to achieve will be achieved.

Don't aim for success if you want it; just do what you love and believe in, and it will come naturally.

- David Frost

AYOKANMI & TOLUWANI BINUTU
Pencils n Brushes Artworks

Pencils n Brushes Artworks (PnB) is a service company in the arts and crafts industry in Nigeria and Africa providing services like Artworks and Design.

PnB which started out in 2010 is a partnership between two brothers, Ayo (Kanmi) and Tolu (wani) Binutu. The brothers decided to have PnB as "a safe haven for like-minded artists to create the most spectacular art forms the world had ever seen".

PnB is dedicated to creating beauty and has created art pieces for a large number of clients who not only love their art, but also believe what they believe: "That regardless of specialty, vocation or hobbies, we should always look to be better today than we were yesterday. There is always a higher rung to reach for. There is always better. There are no limits. Let's; Create. Spectacular!"

Both Kanmi and Tolu are in their 20s. Kanmi studied Economics at the University of Lagos, before bagging a Masters in Economics and Business, from Leeds University Business School. Tolu on the other hand studied Medicine and Surgery at the University of Lagos.

The Interview:

How did the idea for your business come about?

Although, PnB is a partnership, it has grown to be so much more than two people doing what they love. We had always wanted to belong to a family of creative people, people with like minds and abilities. That is the primary reason why we started the company. Pencils n Brushes artworks also own an Art school, called The Hive. At the Hive, we teach artists to create beautiful art, and how to make a living from it.

Ultimately, Pencils n Brushes wants to correct the negative stereotype that defines the average visual artist on the street: an unserious, difficult-to-understand, governed-by-his-emotions person. Artists are professionals and should be viewed as such.

Give the readers some insight into your business?

At Pencils n Brushes, we create visual art. We create pencil art, paintings and graphic designs. We also teach Visual art at The Hive, our Art school.

In your opinion, what do you consider as some of the top skills needed to be a successful entrepreneur?

As an entrepreneur, you have to be willing to sacrifice safety for the possibility of living your life by your own rules. Your first three business ventures might not work out and it might look like you could have put in that time into working for an established organization and climbing up the corporate ladder. But you have to keep going, because it would have all been for nothing if you give up at your lowest point. As an entrepreneur, you also have to be able to see the bigger picture. You will be expected to have all the answers to all the questions and all the solutions to all the problems. Lastly, you need to have a head for numbers and negotiations.

What demographic group would you consider as your key clients?

Our key clients belong to the group of people who appreciate Art enough to purchase or place orders for it. They are usually in the middle or upper socio-economic class, and have an eye for beauty. They are also well-educated, which helps them understand and appreciate the messages behind the works that we do.

What have been some of your challenges and lessons learned from them?

There are unique challenges associated with building a business from scratch, especially if you have to develop your business model also from scratch. PnB shows that Visual Artists, with their unique and strong personalities, can come together and create spectacular art. Anyone who understands how artists like to operate will understand why this is a big deal. We have had to do without money and without adequate sleep in order to see our child (PnB) grow, while ensuring that morale remains high within the company. We have come to see challenges as the bread we eat to get stronger.

In today's challenging world, what do you do to stay on top of the game?

We read; a lot! Books help us see what is possible. We also interact with artists from all over the nation, and abroad too. You see, the thing about Art is that it is inexhaustible. You really cannot get to the bottom of the cookie jar. You just keep reaching and reaching. We also take risks and sometimes, the risks pan out; many times, they don't. You wouldn't believe us if we told you the number of times we have been rejected since we started PnB. It will move you to tears, but you just have to keep moving forward.

What does success mean to you and the best way to achieve long-term success?

For us, success is the unbridled joy on the faces of our clients as we unveil the artwork we created for them. Success is when we watch the participants of the Hive talk excitedly about the strides they are making in Art. Success is the opportunity people give us to help make their happy moments even happier.

The best way that we know to achieve long-term success is to build a team of like-minded people and to build a system that will outlive you.

What has been your most satisfying moment in business?

Our most satisfying moment is every time our clients are happy with our products and services.

How has being an entrepreneur affected your (family) life?

Every day is a PnB day for us. It is more of a lifestyle these days and our family understands. They have been really supportive and we appreciate them very much.

What other sacrifices have you made to be a successful entrepreneur?

Laughs... my brother, just imagine any sacrifice apart from ritual. If you can imagine it, we have sacrificed it.

On average, how many hours do you work per day and what is your typical day like?

We both stay together at the moment, so a typical day starts with us waking up early and discussing the day ahead of us. We talk about the different projects the company is handling and how best to execute them. Then we get ready for the day and start working. To best understand how we operate, we must explain at this point that the company doesn't run like a typical company. We don't run strict 9-5 work hours and we don't require all employees to report to the office every day. We simply make sure everyone knows and understands what he or she is supposed to do. If the artist feels that he is more likely to get his/her creative juices flowing better by staying home and working, we are cool with it, as long as the end-result justifies the method. We encourage this freedom because art, by nature, abhors strict rules. Creativity shines best when it has as little restrictions as professionalism will allow.

Where do you see yourself and business in another 10 years?

10 years from now, Pencils n Brushes artworks will be the go-to place for all things Art and Design.

What are your guiding personal and business principles?

We have two principles that guide all of us at Pencils n Brushes Artworks. The first is 'It's all about progression'. This helps us remember to always improve on ourselves, regardless of how good we get at doing what we do. The second is 'Create Spectacular!' It helps us to know what to do, every single day of our lives.

What is your greatest fear, and how do you manage fear?

We don't have any fears. When negative thoughts try to come in, we push them out. They don't help, so why let them in?

What is your favourite aspect of being an entrepreneur?

What we like about being an entrepreneur the most is the feeling we get when we see that people want what we and the rest of the team have to offer.

Do you have role models and why?

Some of the people that we look up to are Tonye Cole, Dr Cosmas Maduka and Lance Richlin.

What are your hobbies and what do you do to relax?

We read, watch movies and eat (don't judge us!) when we want to relax.

Do you have any favourite quote or saying?

"If you want to create and capture lasting value, don't build an undifferentiated commodity business" - Peter Thiel

What advice or message do you have for young Africans who want to become entrepreneurs?

'Life, your journey and everything it involves, is all about progression,' so do your best each day!

It's not enough to be busy; so are the ants. The question is: What are we busy about?

- Henry David Thoreau

BERNARD KIWIA
Twende

Bernard Kiwia is the Co-founder and Director of Technology of Twende in Tanzania. He also teaches design to secondary school students and community members while also designing and inventing many things, including a drip irrigation kit, solar water heater, and pedal-powered pump. Twende uses locally-available materials, which means these products are a lot more affordable as compared to alternatives and are also more fit for African life.

While most of the imported solar water heaters require a certain type of roof to mount the product, Twende's requires no special roof because it wanted everyone to be able to use it. The products are all designed to perfectly suit the users, especially those in more remote rural communities.

In 2012, Kiwia started Accelerating Innovation & Social Entrepreneurship (AISE), an innovation centre running creative-capacity building workshops, offering mentorship and advising to aspiring innovators. This was later merged with Twende, another innovation centre that uses simple technology solutions.

The Interview:

How did the idea for your business come about?

The idea for Twende came after visiting MIT and meeting other innovators from around the world who inspired me to continue inventing and teaching others how to be creative using a methodology called Creative Capacity Building when I returned to Tanzania. However, there was no good training space in Tanzania, so I started one so people could create and design their own innovations. After all, it's too difficult to take people from Tanzania to MIT, so we needed our own local place for creating products for Tanzania.

Give the readers some insight into your business?

We are running design trainings for secondary school students and community members while also designing our own life-improving products to sell. In addition, we support innovators to take their products to market and start their own businesses selling their innovations.

In your opinion, what do you consider as some of the top skills needed to be a successful entrepreneur?

For me, I don't think you need special skills to be a successful entrepreneur. What is important is to try to solve problems that you really care about and understand - to find ways to combine what you enjoy with what could also help you. For example, if you don't like *chapati* (a type of Tanzanian bread), you can't make a good *chapatti*. You have to be able to test what you make and know whether or not it is getting better. If you don't like *ugali* (another Tanzanian staple), you can't make a good machine to make *ugali*. Because if you really feel like you want to use the machine for yourself, you will make it better. You'll constantly be thinking about how to improve your machine and your love for *ugali* will motivate you to figure out how to solve every new challenge your machine presents.

What demographic group would you consider as your key clients?

When it come to teaching, we work with a diverse group of people, from 15 years old to 45 years old, any gender, and generally Tanzanians. We prefer to teach in Kiswahili, as it is usually the first language for us Tanzanians.

What have been some of your challenges and lessons learned from them?

One of our challenges is consistently procuring materials - they're not always the same and it's difficult to deal with fluctuating prices. Selling products also takes some time, especially to get those first customers. You have to use a lot of energy to convince those first customers to buy your product. What we've realised is people won't trust your product until they use it and see it is working well. So, sometimes we offer contracts where people buy products at half-price, use the product for some time, and later we return to the customer to collect the rest of the money. This gives our customers time to test and confirm that our products work well.

In today's challenging world, what do you do to stay on top of the game?

I observe other people and ask myself: What are they doing? What new products are on the market? What improvements have people made? What can I do to make sure our products compete with the current products on the market?

What does success mean to you and the best way to achieve long-term success?

For me, success is when you think of something, maybe a solution for a challenge you want to solve, and you manage to make it to a point that you feel it is what you were looking for. You have to work hard sometimes and keep thinking of better ways to do your work.

What has been your most satisfying moment in business?

It's been incredible realising something that initially started as an idea - creating a workshop for Tanzanians to make their own technologies - is starting to gain traction. Nowadays, I see a number of Tanzanians really like it, and they keep coming back on their own with their own ideas. Other moments have been satisfying as well, such as taking ideas like the drip irrigation kit and making them into real products we can sell and that can make an impact in the community.

How has being an entrepreneur affected your (family) life?

My parents worked hard to support me in what I'm doing, and my family is very supportive of my work. Through my innovation centre, my family can have their daily bread.

What other sacrifices have you made to be a successful entrepreneur?

Sometimes when you come up with an idea, you don't know if that idea will work. You put in a lot of your money and effort, but sometimes by the end of the day, it's just not going to work. But then you have to go back and think about what's wrong. So sometimes you lose money as you come up with new ideas and try new things. For example, I designed a local bicycle-powered juice blender and used a lot of my energy to make it better and better, but unfortunately, I can no longer find a specific material necessary for production so for now we can't make any more juice blenders. It is hard to feel like I lost all that time, energy, and money I put into the design.

On average, how many hours do you work per day and what is your typical day like?

I work about 8 hours a day, five or six days a week. Normally I get to work around 8 am, have my second breakfast with my colleagues to catch up on their lives, then I proceed to starting or finishing any work and/or inventions I'm working on. To be honest, we don't have any specific schedule as it depends on the day. If you're teaching in school, you follow a schedule, but for us, it depends on the activities going on at that time. Some typical activities include: thinking of innovations, improving innovations already existing, and advising people on their innovations. We also train people, and sometimes this means we visit primary or secondary schools or communities up to 5 hours away from Twende. As the Director of Technology, I have to be flexible, depending on if someone needs help.

Where do you see yourself and business in another 10 years?

In 10 years, we aim to have a number of creative people trained at Twende who have created locally-made products. Also, we hope our innovation centre will have branches around Tanzania, maybe in Morogoro, Mbeya, and/or Mwanza. As for me, I hope to gain fame in Tanzania because I have trained all these people who are making a real impact on society. My students and I will be examples of good local innovators for future generations.

What are your guiding personal and business principles?

It's a challenge, but sometimes you make a plan to start with and then something happens and plans change and you have to adapt. For instance, let's say you intend to buy a new car in 6 months, but you suddenly find a car at a very cheap price. You will buy it immediately because the opportunity presents itself. Sometimes things happen that are not in the plan, but if you see the opening, you should go after it. To make a decision, you should figure out who can help you and how you can organise things. Then you can make an informed decision on how to start and how to proceed.

What is your greatest fear, and how do you manage fear?

Losing my job is my greatest fear, because that is what keeps my family alive. Also, because I have put so much energy into my work, if my centre fails, all my effort has disappeared. I work hard and think of new ideas to keep Twende growing.

What is your favourite aspect of being an entrepreneur?

I can do things for myself and I can run my own business. When you are self-employed, you can make things that you think matters.

Do you have role models and why?

I look to the Chinese for guidance because they make things we should make ourselves. We can come up with more ideas based on looking at their products. They make things that aren't so complicated, which allows other nations like Tanzania to copy the technologies and make them better suited for local settings.

What are your hobbies and what do you do to relax?

I like playing and listening to music. I enjoy listening to stories and occasionally indulge in some drinks ☺

Do you have any favourite quote or saying?

No.

What advice or message do you have for young Africans who want to become entrepreneurs?

There is no simple way of finding success in life. If you want to be a good entrepreneur, you have to work hard and think hard, and you have to do something. There is no shortcut to success. Being a thief might seem like a shortcut, but think about it: you have to stay awake late at night, you have to plan elaborate schemes, and you have to risk your life… In short, there is simply no shortcut to success in life.

Many of life's failures are people who did not realise how close they were to success when they gave up.

- Thomas Edison, inventor and businessman

BETHLEHEM TILAHUN ALEMU
soleRebels Footwear

Antonio Fiorente Photographer

Bethlehem Tilahun Alemu is a woman of many hats. In addition to being the Founder and Chief Executive Officer of soleRebels footwear, she's also the founder/Curator of Republic of Leather, Founder/CEO of Garden of Coffee and founder of Perimeter Consulting.

"My driving passions are sharing Ethiopian cultures with the world , and finding exciting ways to keep these cultures vibrant and fully relevant . "My goal is to build exciting brands around these unique cultures, brands that become as ubiquitous and impactful as APPLE ..."

soleRebels is the world & Africa's fastest-growing footwear brand and the only WFTO Fair Trade footwear company in the world. Its products are carefully handcrafted "by fusing the Ethiopian artisan heritages with fantastic design." Republic of Leather is a super cool company that is changing the way people around the world buy & love luxury leatherwear.

Garden of Coffee is her other gift to the world while her Perimeter Consulting provides strategic consulting services which among others has launched and leads Made By Ethiopia, a groundbreaking public-private partnership that is transforming the entire dynamic of Ethiopia's footwear and leather export sector's , creating over 100,000 new job opportunities and over $1 billion USD in export revenue.

soleRebels is on track to be the first global branded retail chain from a developing nation to open 100 stores and achieve over $200 million USD in revenues by 2019.

On 22 June 2016 Bethlehem made history by becoming the first ever African entrepreneur to ever address the General Assembly at the United Nations Global Leaders Summit. A graduate of Unity University and Harvard University Kennedy School with a Doctorate degree in Commerce, her efforts have brought wide global acclaim and have won numerous honours & awards.

The Interview:

How did the idea for your business come about?

Prior to starting soleRebels, while I was in college, I worked with various companies in the leather and apparel sector in a variety of capacities including marketing and sales, design, and production. This gave me good industry knowledge that was extremely useful in terms of setting up the company and growing it.

However, after working in the private sector for a while I had a strong desire to start to focus my business skills on my community, an improvised area. I knew that there were *so many talented people* there who could do great things if only given a chance. I repeatedly saw what a lot of these people could do in terms of various craft and creative skills. However, owing to extreme poverty, stigma, marginalisation and a whole load of other factors, many of them could not even get simple jobs. This was devastating for me as I grew up with them - they were my neighbours, my family members.

I also saw the devastating effect that aid and charity had on the wider community which made people complacent and dependant. Therefore, I knew that anything that I did for the community had to be truly business-oriented in order to negate the effects that the aid and charity mentality had instilled in many people. The pride that comes with financing ourselves and not waiting for handouts!

I grew up here, completed all my education here in Ethiopia and started soleRebels in my community and have never lived anywhere else but Ethiopia. It's a myth that you have to go outside the country of your birth to be successful, and I'm a proof that it is possible for Africans to build a successful global company while using local resources and starting from the scratch.

What does your success mean to people in general?

My success has served as a powerful counter to generations of media that has attempted to show Ethiopians as helpless passive recipients of aid. My story runs directly counter to that narrative, and has in fact flipped the discourse on African development from one of poverty alleviation orchestrated by external actors, to one about prosperity creation driven by local Africans maximising their talents and resources.

I have shown that it is we Ethiopians and Africans who can create prosperous jobs, world class brands while empowering our communities. And I have done so while presenting a galvanized, dynamic face of African creativity to the global market.

Take us to the beginning of soleRebels

I started soleRebels for two essential reasons:

1. We had lots of talented people in my community, especially artisans, and there were little to no Job opportunities for them. That struck me as both an immense tragedy but at the same time an immense opportunity. Added to this artisan talent was an abundance of natural resources here in Ethiopia from which to craft awesome footwear - everything from free range leathers to organic cottons, jute and Abyssinian hemp - a perfect platform just waiting for something big to happen. So I knew if we could leverage these talents in the correct format, the response from the market would be incredible. We selected footwear as the platform and away we went…

2. Layered on top of this was that I kept hearing over and over the phrase "poverty alleviation" in the wider context of Ethiopia and specifically with regards to the community where I grew up. As I entered college and started working to support myself and my brothers, it had become clear to me that Poverty alleviation is a myth.

It became clear to me that prosperity creation is the sole route to the elimination of poverty. And to create sustained prosperity you have to create something truly world class. So that's what started to really crystallize my thinking.

So, I vowed that I would impact my community in a way that all those who said they were impacting it ever had and never could.

From day 1 we have always said this company is about maximizing local talent and local resources to create good paying jobs.

What have been some of your challenges and lessons learned from them?

Too many challenges to list but as I always say if you are not experiencing ongoing challenges and obstacles then you are not really in a dynamic meaningful business.
An entrepreneur is innovation driven, reliant on the power of their ideas, actions and outputs rather than who their family is, or how good their connections

are or what their market dominance is.

My experience has been no different, but at the end of the day it's the consumer who decides whether or not something is valuable. So once you connect directly and meaningfully with the consumer then they become the arbiter of success as opposed to other factors.

What different soleRebels from others?

I love the fact that soleRebels is *the brand*, the factory, the marketer, the designer, the shipper. It's a radical yet beautifully simple repositioning of the producer consumer paradigm. I love that people can connect with me as the founder and CEO of the company and as the head of customer relations - there's no "hidden executives" or 3rd party layers to reach me - you want me - email me. That's why I answer every single communication we receive from customers myself, be it an order status enquiry, a retailer request for something or a media request!

What is the core attribute of your company?

Each and every soleRebels shoe radiates with what we call the essential 4 C'S; the 4C's is the shorthand we use to guide our design and production process, ensuring that each and every soleRebels shoe posses the core qualities/attributes of: Creativity + Colour + Craftsmanship + Comfort...

It's challenging but anything good is challenging. It requires an obsession with quality, attention to detail, and craftsmanship. soleRebels proudly stands apart and offers a much desired alternative for the informed global consumer.

What is the business model for soleRebels?

Our type of business model centres on eco-sensibility and community empowerment; product design and development involves a great deal of effort to achieve fashionable and appealing quality products that use local materials. Our model maximizes local development by creating a vibrant local supply chain while creating world class footwear that are loaded with style , comfort and appeal.

Where do you see yourself and business in another 10 years?

We have already opened 18 stand alone branded soleRebels retail stores around the world. Our global stores are in: USA, Greece, Taiwan, Japan, Switzerland, Singapore, Austria, Spain, Ethiopia etc.

We plan to open 50 - 60 more soleRebels retail store over the next three years in the markets above and in the US, Canada, Germany, France, Switzerland , China, Hong Kong, Korea, India, Sweden, Norway, Italy, the UK, France, Indonesia, Malaysia, the Philippines, Australia, Kenya, Uganda, Nigeria!

We are on track to open over 150 stores and generate over $ 250 million USD in revenue by 2018, and over 500 global stores and $1 billion in revenues by 2022!

What do you consider as some of the top skills needed to be a successful entrepreneur?

I would like to share what I call the soleRebels 6 point plan for everlasting success:

1. Love your customers; passionately; always. Without them you have nothing!
2. Create truly awesome products that your customers will love; deliver these products with equally awesome customer focused service so your customers will love you in return!
3. Market honestly - no one likes being scammed.
4. Stay agile; never allow complacency; always be eager to examine ALL your assumptions and, if need be, to react immediately if those assumptions come up short.
5. Be open and transparent and above all, be responsive - companies are posting, tweeting all over the place but many never take time to listen and respond when you contact them. C'mon when people ask you a question, answer it - ASAP!

6. Embrace Failure - no one created true awesomeness by being timid; going big means you will fail; *often*. It's what you learn and apply from that failure that will enable you to achieve greatness…

7. Repeat points 1 through 6. Forever!

There's only one thing that makes a dream impossible to achieve: the fear of failure.

- Paulo Coelho, Writer

BIOKU RAHMON JIMOH
Bioraj Pharmaceutical Industries Limited

Rahmon Bioku is the Chairman and Chief Executive Officer of Bioraj Pharmaceutical Industries Limited, a Nigeria indigenous pharmaceutical company.

The company which started operation in 1994 has its manufacturing plant in Ilorin, the capital of Kwara state in the west of the country. The plant has capacity to produce tablets (including blistered one) and syrups. It also has two other outlets, one in Yauri in Kebbi state and the other located in Kwara state as well.

Bioraj Pharmaceutical Industries has over 46 registered products with The

National Agency for Food and Drug Administration and Control (NAFDAC), a Nigerian federal health agency responsible for regulating and controlling the manufacture, importation, exportation, advertisement, distribution, sale and use of food, drugs, cosmetics, medical devices, chemicals and packaged water.

The company is a frequent supplier to major hospitals, various State governments as well as the Federal Ministry of Health.

Bioku, a registered pharmacist in Nigeria and a member of the international pharmaceutical federation is an accomplished merit award winner.

The Interview:

How did the idea for your business come about?

As a Pharmacist who does have interest in working for the government, the ultimate is to be independent by establishing a private enterprise. However, the idea of a pharmaceutical manufacturing company originated in the early eighties when I visited Glaxo Limited, a multinational company. This dream was supported when I did my internship at a university college where I was posted to a unit and was able to get a lot of manufacturing experience.

Give the readers some insight into your business?

We basically produce drugs in different forms - mainly solid and liquid. As at today, we have 46 registered products with the national agency for foods and drugs administration (NAFDAC). We equally have about 15 new products about to be introduced to Nigeria market. Our products are available in all pharmaceutical outlets throughout Nigeria.

In your opinion, what do you consider as some of the top skills needed to be a successful entrepreneur?

To be a successful entrepreneur, one needs to love and enjoy what one does. Have a set goal, be dedicated, get a good team and cultivate the right attitude. There are bound to be challenges but the right frame of mind and attitude and prayers makes them all surmountable.

What demographic group would you consider as your key clients?

The entire Nigerians are our clients.

What have been some of your challenges and lessons learned from them?

Some of them are irregular supply of electricity, lack of easy access to fund, high cost of fund where available and inadequate infrastructure. We have come to the reality of facing the challenges head on and have learnt that only the tough get going when the going gets tough.

In today's challenging world, what do you do to stay on top of the game?

We maintain high quality standard no matter the difficulties.

What does success mean to you and the best way to achieve long-term success?

I do not see success as a measure of wealth accumulation, but rather how many lives have been positively affected by what I do. To achieve a long-term success, one needs to continue to learn and improve on what one does in line with the constantly changing environment.

What has been your most satisfying moment in business?

This was when two of my products won national awards organised by the Institute of Leadership Technology.

How has being an entrepreneur affected your (family) life?

Initially, it was not easy with my immediate family. Today however, thanks to God, my immediate family as well as the entire community that I belong to positively feel the impact of my company.

What other sacrifices have you made to be a successful entrepreneur?

I had to deny myself a lot of pleasure at the early days to save enough funds to move the company ahead.

On average, how many hours do you work per day and what is your typical day like?

Honestly, I do not have a particular working hour, but I ensure that I have enough rest and also create time to play and impact needed knowledge on my children. As a rule, I stay indoors and do not go out after 9 p.m.

Where do you see yourself and business in another 10 years?

In that period, I project to have established World Health Organisation's qualified injection plants.

What are your guiding personal and business principles?

Fear of God in whatever I do.

What is your greatest fear, and how do you manage fear?

I do not have any fear because I do my best and leave the rest to God.

What is your best aspect of being an entrepreneur?

I enjoy being a professional entrepreneur.

Do you have role models and why?

Honestly, I have many and they are too numerous to mention. What I see in one role model may be different from the other. However, my main role model is Prophet Muhammed, may Peace and Blessings of God be with him!

What are your hobbies and what do you do to relax?

I listen to good music and also meditate

Do you have any favourite quote or saying?

Yes I do. 'Do unto others as you want others to do unto you.'

What advice or message do you have for young Africans who want to become entrepreneurs?

They need to be more focused and know that they can also be employer of labour instead of looking for a white collar job.

About the only thing that comes to us without effort is old age.

- Gloria Pitzer, American writer

BITEBO GOGO
Keeping It Real (KIR) Foundation

Bitebo Gogo is the Executive Director of Keeping It Real (KIR) Foundation, KIR Foundation Inclusive Resource and Rehabilitation Community Centre, the only one of its kind in the Niger Delta, Nigeria.

KIR whose vision is to raise innovative leaders committed to lifelong learning to transform their communities. The purpose statement of KIR is 'Inspiring Change Through Learning' with services such as Inclusive Resource Room and Library, Creative Abilities Unit for Persons with Disabilities, Training (ICT, Sign language,

Entrepreneurship / Financial Literacy, Vocational Skills); Support for Autism, Mentoring and Counselling.

Bitebo Gobo earned her law degree from the Rivers State University of Science and Technology, Nigeria and I was called to the Nigerian Bar in 1995. She received her LLM from the same University in 2006 and worked in corporate Nigeria for over 10 years. A chartered Arbitrator and Mediator, she's also a volunteer/patron with the Nigerian Red Cross Society, the Founding Curator of the Port-Harcourt Global Shapers Hub, an initiative of the World Economic Forum, a member of the Board of Experts, AIESEC University of Port-Harcourt and a member of the Technical Committee of the Rivers State Sustainable Development Goals Office.

The Interview:

How did the idea for your business (non-profit) come about?

In 2010, after a life threatening experience, I had an epiphany that I had only one life to live and my life was only worthwhile if I followed my dreams. Kindly watch my TEDx video: 'A Chance to Live Again@A Chance To Live Again.| Bitebo Gogo |TEDxPortHarcourt www.youtube.com/watch?v=OE8pkVwURiw to get more details.

Give the readers some insight into your business (non-profit)?

KIR Foundation is an inclusive non-profit organisation that exists to transform the lives of vulnerable children, youths, persons with disabilities, prison inmates, women and our local communities through Education, Advocacy, Capacity and Sustainable Development.

In the past 5 years, KIR Foundation has invested over $144,000, 00 in 80 institutions in Nigeria (Lagos State, Rivers State, Imo State and Abuja the capital of Nigeria), making a difference in the lives of more than 16,000 beneficiaries by donating over 12,342 books, educational aids, starter kits and farming implements and publishing a 'The Young Leader's Guide, a leadership manual for young people.

In your opinion, what do you consider as some of the top skills needed to be a successful (social) entrepreneur?

Leadership especially that of servant leadership, empathy, constructive passion, optimism, innovation and creativity, grit, emotional and social intelligence, communication skills, resilience, a collaborative spirit and teachability.

What demographic group would you consider as your key clients (Beneficiaries or stakeholders)?

Vulnerable children, youths, persons with disabilities, prison inmates, women and local communities.

What have been some of your challenges and lessons learned from them?

Identifying the needs of the beneficiaries, creating opportunities for the beneficiaries that are sustainable, getting beneficiaries to take ownership of projects, getting stakeholder buy in especially those in charge of the beneficiaries, accomplishing a win-win situation with stakeholders with regards to what is in it for them, developing the capacity of staff and beneficiaries, managing hostility from beneficiaries and stakeholders, environmental and financial constraints (especially trying to maintain our policy of investing 60% of general donations in projects and 100% of project donations in projects without compromising or effectiveness and efficiency.

In today's challenging world, what do you do to stay on top of the game?

Deep faith in God, taking care of myself (quiet moments, exercising, eating right, sleeping well), having a strong support structure (family friends, board, a great team, volunteers and stakeholders), continuous learning, collaboration, deliberately and proactively building sustainable structures, reputation and social capital, lean budgeting without compromising global standards and staffing ones' weaknesses either by delegating or outsourcing, consistently improving and creating opportunities.

What does success mean to you and the best way to achieve long-term success?

Success is being at peace with God and knowing that I am better than who I was yesterday. The best way to achieve long term success is to become the better version of myself every day in all my various roles.

What has been your most satisfying moment in business (non-profit)?

Seeing that our beneficiaries are becoming self sufficient or interdependent, that our projects/initiatives are sustainable and staff and volunteers are experiencing personal growth.

How has being a social entrepreneur affected your (family) life?

The difficulty in achieving work life balance, my work is my calling; therefore it is an integral part of my life. Unfortunately, one will miss out on certain moments. However, wherever I am at any moment, I deliberately enjoy the moment.

What other sacrifices have you made to be a successful social entrepreneur?

I have not earned a salary in five years in order to continuously grow KIR Foundation, and have had to give up some of my privacy and most weekends.

On average, how many hours do you work per day and what is your typical day like?

Usually 10-12 hours; however on the days that I have meetings with stakeholders it could be 15 or more. Meetings, coaching and mentoring, fund raising, supervising and working on documents and responding to mails.

Where do you see yourself and business (Non-profit) in another 10 years?

I would like to go back to school and get a masters degree in development practice, work with an International Donor Agency. KIR Foundation would have its own property, set up an inclusive start-up hub and set-up a sustainable social enterprise.

What are your guiding personal and business principles?

Deep faith in God, commitment to family, continual growth; add value to those around me and excellence.

What is your greatest fear, and how do you manage fear?

Failing to please God and living below my potentials. I get back up again, rely on God when I fall and constantly improve myself.

What is your best aspect of being a social entrepreneur?

Making a positive difference in the world.

Do you have role models and why?

The Lord Jesus Christ; the Late Selwyn Hughes for their humility and compassion for humanity and John Maxwell, for developing leaders,

What are your hobbies and what do you do to relax?

Reading, writing, coaching and mentoring; travelling for self development, discussing with cerebral minded people, attending book readings, conferences and artistic shows.

Do you have any favourite quote or saying?

Romans 8:28 - All things work together for good. Also, one by Steve Jobs that, "You can't connect the dots looking forward; you can only connect them looking backwards. So you have to trust that the dots will somehow connect in your future."

What advice or message do you have for young Africans who want to become social entrepreneurs?

Transformative world change must start with you; become solution minded and think of creative ways that you can add value to the lives of those around you, then become a volunteer in the area of your passion and if you are convinced that you want to start a non- profit organisation, just do it and never stop learning or making a difference!

In helping others, we shall help ourselves, for whatever good we give out completes the circle and comes back to us.

- Flora Edwards, American author

CARINE-ZOE UMUTONI
ONYX

Carine Umutoni Zoe, the young Founder and Chief Executive Office of ONYX is a budding fashion designer and entrepreneur based in Kigali, Rwanda.

"I am a proud Rwandan. I love my country and what's actually happening after going through the genocide. "I have lived my life outside the country for many years with my family. "I lived in South Africa for nearly 8 years, but have decided to come back home and serve my community."

The Interview:

How did the idea for your business come about?

The idea came to me since I was a child. I have always liked to design and I must say it's probably a given talent. I have decided to use my talents to bless the world and get paid for it.

My Mother played a very big role in this as she once told me: "Carine, use your talents and God will indeed bless you for it. Consider it and turn it into business and this will sustain you". That was it! After being frustrated, working as a Communication Expert, I ended up resigning and that was my turning point.

Give the readers some insight into your business?

I design clothes using pure cotton and adding an African touch to it, like embroidery and nice African pieces to make it unique. My brand is called ZAA Designs which means rebirth.

In your opinion, what do you consider as some of the top skills needed to be a successful entrepreneur?

I will say determination and loyalty to your business idea.

What demographic group would you consider as your key clients?

My key clients are international and expatriates within my country and outside.

What have been some of your challenges and lessons learned from them?

To pursue my dream and decide to be loyal even when I see nothing happening. I have learnt that business has many facets and sometimes one is surprised by the outcomes but one should keep marching on because there are many big and huge rewards ahead.

In today's challenging world, what do you do to stay on top of the game?

I am ME and I give what I have which is my authentic Me. Being creative is one. I use simplicity and more of a storytelling in my designs. You see, in my designs you get to know me as a person because I design what I have within me and invite the world to come into my world.

What does success mean to you and the best way to achieve long-term success?

Success is being able to share the best of yourself to bless your family, community, country and the rest of the world. Serving others is Success!

What has been your most satisfying moment in business?

Liaising with my clients and making profits as I move forward.

How has being an entrepreneur affected your (family) life?

They support me and they are also inspired to start their own business.

What other sacrifices have you made to be a successful entrepreneur?

Is to leave my comfort zone; leaving my work was one of the major sacrifice I have had to make.

On average, how many hours do you work per day and what is your typical day like?

I work from 8:00 a.m. to 7:00 p.m. I read my emails first and respond immediately. Being professional is replying to important emails immediately. Then I go to the factory and work with the tailors for the upcoming trade shows or orders from my clients.

Where do you see yourself and business in another 10 years?

I will be among the top 5 women that have changed the economy of Africa. Oh yes, it's my wish and of course, this will require strength and working hard. My company will be known as the most successful of all time, not only in sales but in having employed and changed people's lives all around the world.

What are your guiding personal and business principles?

My principle is to always stay true to myself and be loyal to my business ideals.

What is your greatest fear, and how do you manage fear?

I pray and talk to God about my weaknesses.

What is your best aspect of being an entrepreneur?

Being independent and deciding for yourself and redirecting your brand and make it what you want it to be.

Do you have role models and why?

Yes my role model is Oprah Winfrey. She is a strong Black woman who stands tall for what she believes in. It's my wish to meet her one day. My number one model of all times is my President, His Excellency President Paul Kagame of Rwanda. His determination and wisdom has got us as Rwandans thus far.

What are your hobbies and what do you do to relax?

I love spa and eating out on weekends. Reading books as well and hanging out with my family does it for me.

Do you have any favourite quote or saying?

One by Maya Angelou: I have learned that "People will forget what you said. People will forget what you did. But people will never forget how you made them feel."

What advice or message do you have for young Africans who want to become entrepreneurs?

Trust in yourself and not let the world dictate to you. Be loyal to your dreams and shine. Nobody can believe in you if you do not believe in yourself. Believing in yourself is the first step. The sky is the limit!

We must all suffer one of two things: the pain of discipline or the pain of regret and disappointment.

- Jim Rohn, Entrepreneur and Motivational Speaker

CAROLINE WANJIKU
Daproim Africa

Caroline Wanjiku, a social entrepreneur, is the Chief Executive Officer of Daproim Africa, an organisation operating in the Business Process Outsourcing space, based in Nairobi, Kenya.

Daproim's stated mission is to provide high quality IT enabled business solutions geared towards delivering positive social transformational impact to African youth. It employs 100 full time staff and 400 part time university students from vulnerable communities.

Wanjiku who holds two MBA degrees in Strategic Management and Entrepreneurial Leadership from University of Nairobi and Portland States University is a member of YWSE Nairobi (Young women social entrepreneurs) and Cherie Blair Foundation for Women.

The Interview:

How did the idea for your business come about?

Daproim Africa started as a dream after the founder, the late Steve Muthee decided to test the hypothesis of his campus research paper on financial outsourcing. Having cleared campus and tried his hands on a job or two, he decided he is better venturing into business. He started by doing online jobs with 2 employees; himself and his best friend and the rest is history filled with Gods favour and hard work. We are now employing hundreds of youth every year. His story was very interesting; wish I had the time to share it.

Give the readers some insight into your business including groups we consider our clients?

Daproim Africa is a business processing and outsourcing social enterprise providing quality and affordable volume data management services to local and international research firms, governments, academic and medical institutions, media companies, telecoms and corporations.

Our services are diverse; from offering complete end-to-end digitization services (scanning, indexing , providing document management systems (DMS) that help companies better manage and use data) to providing transcription services to customer support services which include both online and telephone support to content creation, data mining and analysis and Data Entry services. Daproim also provides IT services like Desktop/Web/Mobile Applications, Desktop Publishing and Photo editing and Geographic Information Systems.

In your opinion, what do you consider as some of the top skills and traits needed to be a successful entrepreneur?

Passionate about the business, humility and fierce resolve, learning spirit, competence, courageous, focused and committed, positive attitude, resilient, peoples focused.

What have been some of your challenges and lessons learned from them?

Our kind of work mostly experiences technical challenges but we have been able to mitigate these by investing in state of the art infrastructure. Penetrating the local market has also been a challenge but we have invested in consumer education to build a case for our services.

In today's challenging world, what do you do to stay on top of the game?

We have a unique selling proposition; we not only sell quality but also impact. Organisations want to be associated with brands that contribute to the positive change. When our clients associate an impact story directly to their organisation outsourcing work to our company, they give us more work and even offer to pay slightly more for the impact we create. We have great testimonials and references from clients who are extremely happy with our work. Lastly, keeping up with the industry trends and being trend setters, extensive marketing to our target niche and consumer education has supported our efforts.

What does success mean to you and the best way to achieve long-term success?

Success for me is two way. One is impact, the difference we create in the lives of young people from poor communities that we employ in our company. Just seeing they can earn an extra dollar to support their families, to enrol to that course they have always wanted to do or move to a better house. Two, success to us is a happy client and valuable lessons learnt as we implement different projects. Every time we complete a project, we are keen on feedback from the client. We are keen to ensure that the client is not only satisfied with the results but the process and people we used to get the work done.

For us, the best way to achieve long term success is to continuously challenge our company's status quo and reinvent ourselves in the areas of process, people and impact.

What has been your most satisfying moment in business?

On the business front, working with companies like WIPO, being recognised as change agents by foundations like the Rockefeller Foundation gave us confidence to continue doing what we do best, providing quality services while impacting lives.

On the social front, each day we have an impact story of hope, of transformed lives brings satisfaction to us - knowing that we contribute to something more than business growth.

How has being an entrepreneur affected your (family) life?

My family is part of my entrepreneurial journey. I have had to be intentional to ensure I manage my time properly so I don't miss out on my family. For me business and family are the same; if I have to get results, I have to invest time, effort and money to make both business and family work. I am frantic about growing the business as I am about being there for my family. Of course there are moments when I think about business when I'm with family and I have to answer to urgent emails/ calls when family needs my attention but that's the life of an entrepreneur.

What other sacrifices have you made to be a successful entrepreneur?

I would say sleep and social life. In as much as I have tried to preserve healthy sleeping habits and social networks, I have had to sacrifice some sleep and time with my friends to get proposals together, travel for business, make it to a meeting or get tasks done. Sometimes its nights spend away wondering and strategizing about the future of the company.

On average, how many hours do you work per day and what is your typical day like?

Being the strategic leader of my company, I invest more time in building and managing the business. Sometimes, I invest close to 14 hours a day, sometimes less. I wake up at 5am every morning and go to bed after 9pm. My typical day includes working out in the morning or evening, attending to meetings, either strategy, pitching or relationship building (networking), goal setting and reviewing progress and communicating to world. I have learnt to work with a to-do-list to get work done. I also make sure I spend some quality time with my daughter.

Where do you see yourself and business in another 10 years?

Every time I think of Daproim, I think of Africa and how my company can change Africa (people and processes). In line with our mission and strategic plan, I see myself leading an Africa company with foot prints in 5 African countries providing quality service with a passion and positively affecting the lives of 20,000 young people.

What are your guiding personal and business principles?

My guiding personal and business principle is centred on integrity, showing up at the right time, doing the right thing, with the right people and proper resources.

What is your greatest fear, and how do you manage fear?

The world is changing very fast, every day I wake-up, there is some new process, new technology, new business. My greatest challenge is remaining relevant amidst changing times. Being at the fore front of what is happening in the IT sector in terms of seeking knowledge, researching and building networks has helped me manage some of that fear.

What is your best aspect of being an entrepreneur?

The best part of being an entrepreneur is to hear our customers tell us how we have changed their lives and impacted their businesses. I enjoy sharing my vision and excitement for the future of the company and seeing that manifested in the contagious passion of our employees. I enjoy the relationships I have built with my employees and clients but mostly other entrepreneurs that share agonies, experiences and successes.

Do you have role models and why?

I have a couple of role models because I believe for me to be a successful entrepreneur I need to understand and emulate some of their journeys that inspire me to behave in ways that contribute to my success.

What are your hobbies and what do you do to relax?

I enjoy travelling and sightseeing. To relax, I play with my daughter and sometimes enjoy a day at the Spa.

Do you have any favorite quote or saying?

"If somebody offers you an amazing opportunity but you are not sure you can do it, say yes, and then learn how to do it later!" - *Richard Branson*

"The biggest risk is not taking any risk. In a world that's changing really quickly, the only strategy that is guaranteed to fail is not taking risks." - *Mark Zuckerberg*

"There's lot of bad reasons to start a company. But there's only one good, legitimate reason, and I think you know what it is: it's to change the world." - Phil Libin, CEO of Evernote.

What advice or message do you have for young Africans who want to become entrepreneurs?

The world needs new entrepreneurs every day to innovate, deliver solutions, create jobs, lift the standard of living, usher new technology into society, and keep competition alive in the marketplace. Successful entrepreneurship requires passion, action, commitment, consistency, courage, clarity and mentorship. Lastly, adopt a Mentor! And pray.

I never dreamed about success. I worked for it.

- Estee Lauder, American businesswoman

CHARLES COOPER & MLEN-TOO WESLEY
Cookshop

Cookshop, an online platform allows customers to order food from nearly all the major restaurants in Liberia.

It is the brainchild of two U.S. educated ICT professionals, Charles Dorme Cooper and Mlen-Too Wesley.

Charles Dorme Cooper has over 15 years of experience in branding, marketing, graphic design and web development while Mlen-Too Wesley specializes in software engineering and network administration. They both returned to Liberia in 2010 to play a role in the post-war reconstruction of the country.

It's a simple and convenient business model that allows users to browse the menu online, select food and place order. The order is processed by Cookshop who then automatically contact the vendor/restaurant. Depending on the selected choice, the order can be delivered right at the doorstep of the customer or pick-up after an order-ready-alert is sent through a seamless automated SMS service.

It's a win-win situation for Cookshop, the participating restaurants as well as customers. The restaurants now enjoy higher sales and less hassles while busy customers can have their food delivered to them at any location of choice or have a ready-to-go meal picked up.

The Interview:

How did the idea for your business come about?

We wanted to create a new Liberian story of innovation and entrepreneurship driven by local investment, and to set an example for other local entrepreneurs in our generation. After studying the local market, we realised that professionals often don't have the time to discover the food options available to them. nor to stop what they are doing to go and grab the meal when they are hungry. We created Cookshop to resolve this by aggregating the menus of the best food vendors and combining that with a convenient delivery service.

Give the readers some insight into your business?

Cookshop.biz is an online platform that let users order food from the best restaurants in Monrovia via a mobile device or computer. We are Liberia's first DOT-COM company, and the online destination for food in Liberia.

In your opinion, what do you consider as some of the top skills needed to be a successful entrepreneur?

Entrepreneurs need to have the vision to see opportunities in their market, the faith that their vision can be achieved, and the determination to make the vision a reality. In today's marketplace it helps to be tech savvy as technology solutions can greatly increase efficiency of operations in any kind of business. It also helps to have knowledge of the accounting processes required to operate a business.

What demographic group would you consider as your key clients?

Our key clients are professionals working in Monrovia, the capital city of Liberia.

What have been some of your challenges and lessons learned from them?

Funding and support - We are experiencing exponential growth due to high adoption among our target consumers. But we have reached a point where we need investment in order to truly reach our potential, as we are currently forced to limit our expansion to match our ability to meet demand. Unfortunately there are limited investment resources for small businesses in our market and even less for tech start-ups. Also the business environment and regulations can make it difficult for SMEs to conduct business.

Infrastructure - Liberia has a notoriously unreliable and costly infrastructure. Not only do we have to work around constant power and water outages, we also have to pay a premium cost for those basic utilities.

Hi-Speed Internet - Though the ISPs in Liberia have made many strides towards providing better internet service, they suffer regular outages and internet speeds are often slower than advertised. A dependable source of hi-speed Internet would be a great resource for Cookshop and our customers.

Behaviour change - Cookshop represents a paradigm shift within the market as the first local content provider to provide daily value to our users. Prior to our service, consumers were forced to call in to restaurants to place orders, and then either go to the restaurant, or send someone to pick up their food. Now consumers are conditioned to go online to place their order and have it delivered. This is a result of a targeted and consistent marketing campaign, and a user acquisition strategy that required specific knowledge of the market. We are soon enabling online payment options which will once again represent a paradigm shift in the local market.

Ebola crisis - We launched Cookshop in February 2014 just as the Ebola crisis was unfolding in the region, and by September 2014 we were forced to shut down due to safety concerns. Re-launching our business in July of 2015 required reinvestment and a leap of faith which has paid off immeasurably.

In today's challenging world, what do you do to stay on top of the game?

We try to pay attention to our users by collecting feedback through multiple channels, and since we are a small business we can react quickly using that feedback to improve our service.

We identified our target audience and speak to them directly with consistent messaging via email, SMS and printed promotional material. We also keep an online presence at Facebook, Twitter, Google+, WhatsApp, and Tumblr.

What does success mean to you and the best way to achieve long-term success?

Success is turning your vision into a sustainable reality.

What has been your most satisfying moment in business?

Our most satisfying moment to date was delivering our 10,000th order in early 2016. That moment was proof that Cookshop has more than risen to meet the challenges set before us. Currently, we have completed over 15,000 orders and have over 2,000 users.

How has being an entrepreneur affected your (family) life?

Being an entrepreneur requires a lot of commitment and often keeps you working late. We have been fortunate to have people in our lives that understand our level of commitment to Cookshop.

What other sacrifices have you made to be a successful entrepreneur?

We could be pursuing careers that would be more financially lucrative in the short term.

On average, how many hours do you work per day and what is your typical day like?

Cookshop is open from 9am to 9pm daily (12pm to 9pm on Sundays). We usually work an average of 12 to 14 hours a day.

Where do you see yourself and business in another 10 years?

We intend to expand Cookshop to regional markets in the next 5 years.

What are your guiding personal and business principles?

We believe in hard work and perseverance, backed by research and evidence, to further achievement. We have faith that our actions and path will lead us to success.

What is your greatest fear, and how do you manage fear?

We live in a volatile economy and our greatest fear is that an unexpected event occurs which may affect our business negatively. We prepare for the unexpected by diversifying our revenue sources.

What is your best aspect of being an entrepreneur?

It's a blessing to be able to build your own business instead of someone else's.

Do you have role models and why?

Our role models are entrepreneurs who have impacted the world by meeting the needs in their own communities. Our hope is to also become role models ourselves for the next generation of young Liberian and West African tech entrepreneurs.

What are your hobbies and what do you do to relax?

We are avid readers in our free time. As an entrepreneur you have to keep reading to keep growing. We are also foodies so luckily we get to combine our passion with our business.

Do you have any favourite quote or saying?

A little rain each day will fill the rivers to overflowing. - Liberian Proverb

What advice or message do you have for young Africans who want to become entrepreneurs?

We encourage young entrepreneurs to strive to differentiate their businesses within their local market.

Formal education will make you a living; self-education will make you a fortune.

- Jim Rohn, Entrepreneur & Motivational Speaker

COLIN THORNTON
Dial a Nerd

Dial a Nerd, a South African IT Support company started in a garage in 1998. It has now evolved into an industry leader, a highly professional IT consultancy with branches in Johannesburg and Cape Town.

It's highly technical team provide seamless IT support for Educational Institutions, professional firms and SME. It also provides on-site and off-site IT support for home users and small businesses with vast range of services that include network architecture design to managed services.

Dial a Nerd: "Outsourcing is a strategic tool that can have a powerful positive impact on organisation's focus, growth, financial stability and productivity levels; therefore, concentrate on running your business knowing that your IT infrastructure requirements are being dealt with by highly skilled professionals at a fraction of the cost of an internal IT department."

Colin Thornton is the Founder and current Co-Managing Director.

The Interview:

How did the idea for your business come about?

In 1998, when I started, there were almost no IT Support companies focused on home users. I was always tinkering with computers and would often get asked to help friends and family with their IT problems. They had no idea who else to ask. I did some searching in the phonebook (this was pre-Google) and realised that there was a gap in the market which needed filling. I promptly (much to the dismay of my parents) dropped out of University and started a company. It didn't have a name until my girlfriend at the time jokingly said it should be "Dial a Nerd" - and it stuck!

Give the readers some insight into your business?

Since the days when we were entirely focused on home users we now have two distinct divisions: one for home users and one for businesses. The needs of these two target markets vary greatly so we have different resources, skills and processes set up accordingly. Our main 'product' regardless of the customer is still service.

In your opinion, what do you consider as some of the top skills needed to be a successful entrepreneur?

It's almost a cliché but entrepreneurs need to be able to fail, learn from the failure, adapt and then try again. Sometimes over and over again. The ability to adapt is as important as the ability to keep trying.

What demographic group would you consider as your key clients?

On our Home support side our clients are high LSM individuals and families. On the Business support side it is any business with between 5 and 300 users.

What have been some of your challenges and lessons learned from them?

One challenge we are constantly aware of is that our core business… what we do behind the scenes… is a mystery to many of our customers. And they don't want (and shouldn't have) to understand it. So the challenge is explaining things in a way which is (a) understandable and (b) relevant to the customers' specific needs.

In today's challenging world, what do you do to stay on top of the game?

Always keep our customers' needs in focus. It's very easy to get caught up in the many aspects involved in running a business but you need to keep coming back to the question "Are our customers happy?"

What does success mean to you and the best way to achieve long-term success?

Success to me, in the business world, means having a business which is autonomous. A business shouldn't rely on one person or people to survive. I would consider it a huge achievement and long-term success if Dial a Nerd carried on running regardless of who is a part of it.

What has been your most satisfying moment in business?

I can't identify a specific moment but it is always extremely satisfying when I meet new people and they already know about Dial a Nerd and what we do. Somehow we seem to have managed to get our brand out there very successfully.

How has being an entrepreneur affected your (family) life?

It's very important to have a balance between work and life and, although I don't always get it right, I try my utmost. I'd like to think that being an entrepreneur hasn't negatively impacted this balance although there are occasionally bursts of activity that keep me at the office, and away from my family, longer than usual.

What other sacrifices have you made to be a successful entrepreneur?

Entrepreneurs don't really get holidays. And nowadays with the ubiquitous technology that keeps you connected this is even more true than usual. I'm embarrassed to say that I was still on email throughout my honeymoon. I don't regret it though and often say that I'd probably be more stressed if I wasn't connected all the time - I'd rather know what's going on, even if it's bad news.

On average, how many hours do you work per day and what is your typical day like?

My average work day nowadays is 9 to 10 hours. Back when I started it was much more. I am unfortunately glued to my computer for most part of the day. We rely massively on email and I get hundreds every day which need attention.

Where do you see yourself and business in another 10 years?

I don't think I'll be running the business in 10 years but I'm sure it will still be going strong and constantly evolving. So it'd be very difficult to guess what it's going to look like. We have changed radically in the last five years to match the market and I'm sure that will happen at least a couple more times in the next decade. Technology is progressing so quickly and Dial a Nerd needs to be able to adapt with it at all times.

What are your guiding personal and business principles?

In both aspects I like to challenge myself. So I deliberately try and make some big, almost risky, decisions a couple of times a year and then try and cope with the consequences.

What is your best aspect of being an entrepreneur?

The freedom to create my own destiny.

Do you have role models and why?

I don't really have specific role models but one person who springs to mind is Jim Collins who has written a number of books on business which I really enjoy. He's done a lot of research and then summed it up beautifully.

What are your hobbies and what do you do to relax?

I love the outdoors and try to get out as often as possible. The bush, mountains, rivers and beach!

Do you have any favourite quote or saying?

"Shoot bullets before cannonballs" by Jim Collins. You'll need to read his book "Great by Choice" to understand!

What advice or message do you have for young Africans who want to become entrepreneurs?

Do what you love and put in the hard work. Too many entrepreneurs seem to start businesses just because they have a good idea or product or think they've discovered a niche in the market. However if it's not something you love to do then it's much more difficult to get through the tough times, of which there will probably be many. I believe someone starting a business they love, even in a saturated market, has a greater chance of success. You just need to be better than your competitors and that's easier if you can't wait to get to work in the morning.

Your days are numbered. Use them to throw open the windows of your soul to the sun. If you do not, the sun will soon set, and you with it.

- Marcus Aurelius, Emperor

DANSON MUCHEMI
JamboPay

32-year-old Danson Muchemi is the founder and Chief Executive Officer of JamboPay, an innovative electronic payment services provider in Africa.

The Kenya based JamboPay allow users to securely make and receive payments through mobile phone over internet.

As a result of its quality service, it has succeeded in obtaining several lucrative contracts from public as well as private institutions, including patronage from some governments.

JamboPay: "The gateway has extensively harnessed the existing local and international money transfer solutions to ensure that all visitors are well catered for. The reporting tools that JamboPay provides adequately help in decision making hence productivity in business."

The Interview:

How did the idea for your business come about?

We wanted to create an e-commerce portal for farmers in Kenya in 2008. Halfway into the project we realised there was no payment gateway in Kenya then and we had to build our own. Our efforts to create a payment gateway kicked off. We soon realised that a lot of efforts, infrastructure, regulations and compliance were required for that. We thus decided to shelve our earlier plans on e-commerce portal and instead focused on the payment gateway. We ended up providing the gateway services to other e-commerce service providers. Over time we iterated to include retail (over the counter) payments processing, bank based transaction processing, mobile payments and other payment technologies in response to market needs.

Give the readers some insight into your business?

JamboPay enables consumers/customers to securely pay for goods and services from businesses, governments and other organisations through mobile, web, banks and a network of agents. We enable businesses and governments to securely accept payments from anywhere over web, mobile, banks and agents. We provide the electronic payments as a service.

In your opinion, what do you consider as some of the top skills needed to be a successful entrepreneur?

I think skills can be as diverse as world population but character and qualities necessary are few- mainly. Focus, Patience, Persistence, integrity and hard work.

What demographic group would you consider as your key clients?

Everyone anywhere in the world can use our services to make payments to merchants in Kenya, Uganda, Tanzania, Rwanda and very soon in

Senegal. Businesses in these countries can use our services.

What have been some of your challenges and lessons learned from them?

From the onset we had limited capital. We started very small and in a cyber café in Nairobi. We operated for 6 months in the Café where we rented a computer for $45 a month. Lesson here for all is - Start with what you have, Start Now, keep going. We could not hire strong people in our early days due to financial limitations and I ended up working so hard to cover for the weaknesses. We now have a good and strong team. This has made work easier and fun for everyone. Entrepreneurs have difficulties in letting go of the businesses and certain roles and duties. I had same challenge but my Chairman Hans Brugmans taught me to let go. I have learnt to delegate to the right people and relax. We were poor in record keeping in our first year and that cost us a lot. I have learnt to keep records. I advise young entrepreneurs to keep proper records from day one. Records are better than money in the bank. Proper records are your business' thermometer.

In today's challenging world, what do you do to stay on top of the game?

Stay hungry. Challenge things, people and situations. Challenge everything. Stay grounded and in touch with the society and various stakeholders. Stick to your strategy but keep evaluating it against changes happening. Read right material and most important take care of your body /health. Your health is your biggest asset. I also pray a lot. I would never leave my home to work without a prayer. In other words I win my battles very early ☺

What does success mean to you and the best way to achieve long-term success?

Success is ability to cause a positive change in other people's lives. It is the ability to challenge yourself continuously. Best way to achieve long term success is setting right goals in life. Working towards goals that have the overcoming social problems as measurable deliverables.

What has been your most satisfying moment in business?

Every morning when I interact with my colleagues as they take their seats in the office, I feel I have inspired them to join me towards a common goal. I feel good every time I see clients using our services and realising efficiencies and growths directly attributable to our services. It feels satisfying to create a brand.

How has being an entrepreneur affected your (family) life?

I have spent a lot of time on the business and that time would have probably gone to family.

What other sacrifices have you made to be a successful entrepreneur?

Biggest sacrifice has been time. We have had to let go of many opportunities that are not aligned to our core values such as Integrity.

On average, how many hours do you work per day and what is your typical day like?

I worked up to 15 hours a day 6 and a half days a week in our first year. I even worked half day on Christmas day in 2009. I now work about 9 hours a day for 5 days in a week, I occasionally take time off for holidays. I am up by 0430hrs and go to bed by midnight. My working days are punctuated by lots of meetings. I love food and so Lunch hour is my best hour!

Where do you see yourself and business in another 10 years?

God willing, with our hard work, JamboPay will be a global brand in all continents. We will be a necessity for over 600 million users. I will be developing my next social impact enterprise in 10 years - probably in Biotechnology

What are your guiding personal and business principles?

I am here to cause a change. Everyone in my life is here for me to impact on positively. Life is not to be taken too seriously but work is not to be joked with.

What is your greatest fear, and how do you manage fear?

I fear rats ☺ I try to avoid certain places. My greatest fear in business is complacency and what will be of our industry in future. I try to stay as hungry for challenges as possible. I visit my rural home regularly to remind myself of the social problems that we must tackle as a business.

What is your best aspect of being an entrepreneur?

I can make decisions that can impact positively on lives and communities. We build classrooms for school kids as an obligation and because we can. A world ran by good entrepreneurs could be sustainable world. We never want the cycle to end.

Do you have role models and why?

I have my mother first, she is so strong to have had to educate us and shape us single handedly after Dad passed away. Industrialist Manu Chandaria who has had a lot of impact in our society. He is a believer of Corporate Social responsibility as an obligation. He has taken time to mould his family; you can see that in his Son Darshan.

What are your hobbies and what do you do to relax?

Playing Chess is my hobby. I love travelling.

Do you have any favourite quote or saying?

"When you eat a banana, remember the farmer who planted it."

What advice or message do you have for young Africans who want to become entrepreneurs?

Time to do it is now. How to do it is "Perfectly" Let no one tell you that you cannot make it. That is a lie. The truth is - You are a Champion!

Nothing ever gets easier. You just get stronger.

- Unknown

DONALD BAMBARA
Green' Act

The Green' Act, a social enterprise was born in 2013 when Stéphen Meister, a Swiss exchange student, had the idea to start separating waste at the Institut Supérieur de Management in Dakar. Coming from country with a highly functioning waste management in place, it was very apparent to her that Senegal has a lot of room for improvement in this regard. What better place to start sensitizing people to littering and educate them about recycling than at university?

Together with Donald Patrick Bambara (Burkina Faso), Yannick Gounogbe (Cote d'Ivoire) and four other students, she launched a waste separation system at ISM, collecting plastic separately from other waste in order to sell it to the recycling industry.

Green' Act not only provides places for ISM students to separate trash from recyclable materials, but also educate them through conferences and clean-up sessions on the necessity of doing so.

Green' Act has grown ever since thanks to its supportive network of partner institutions and volunteers. It has won the Sustainable Campus International Competition 2013 and was a finalist in the Anzisha Prize Competition 2013. Green' Act has now extended to other institutions and work in collaboration with key plastic collection and recycling operation.

Bambara who is currently pursuing an MBA programme in China said: *"I believe in Africa's potential of economic and social development thanks to the ambitious youth of this continent. "It is our responsibility to shape our countries for the better and the sooner we seize development opportunities the brighter the future of Africa. The recycling sector bears great economic and ecologic opportunities for Senegal which is why I got involved with Green'Act."*

The Interview:

How did the idea for your business come about?

It all started when I was an undergraduate student at the Institut Superieur de Management in Dakar, Senegal. 7 other friends and I from different parts of the continent wanted to start an innovative social business solving practical issues in Africa. A Swiss, Stephanie Meister was part of our team. She noticed that there is a huge gap in waste management systems between Europe and Africa. In Senegal, we didn't 'have these separated bins and recycling system in campuses and students didn't have a clue about its importance. An educational institution is supposed to shape the next generations of leaders; hence, it is at the upmost importance that these students know and care about the environment and sustainable waste management practices. This is how Green'Act started!

Give the readers some insight into your business?

Initially, Green'Act mission was to bring sustainability into African campuses, from waste management practices to sustainable development curriculum. Today, we are operating as a sustainability advisory firm. Our services ranges from programmes development and implementation support to sustainable strategies design and implementation.

In your opinion, what do you consider as some of the top skills needed to be a successful entrepreneur?

This is a tricky question. However, I believe the key aspect of being an entrepreneur is to have passion to solve a real problem in your community. You need to be passion driven and not money driven.

What demographic group would you consider as your key clients?

They are the educational institutions, public institutions, non-profit organisations and corporations.

What have been some of your challenges and lessons learned from them?

When you want to run your business successfully, it is a key to listen to your clients and to identify what they want. Remember, it is not about you, it is about them.

In today's challenging world, what do you do to stay on top of the game?

I pray and I surround myself with positive people.

What does success mean to you and the best way to achieve long-term success?

Success to me is to achieve what you set out for yourself as personal goals. It also means being able to impact positively to your community and to people's lives.

What has been your most satisfying moment in business?

Impacting people's lives with what I do.

How has being an entrepreneur affected your (family) life?

The support I get from people I surround myself with have taught me as an entrepreneur to aim for the highest target and to go beyond my limits.

What other sacrifices have you made to be a successful entrepreneur?

I could have been doing something that offer more financial reward, stability and with stable pay checks.

On average, how many hours do you work per day and what is your typical day like?

Honestly, I just work until the job needed to be done is done. My day usually start with a great breakfast (the best meal of the day) and a morning prayer which gives me the energy to go through the challenges of the day.

Where do you see yourself and business in another 10 years?

I will still continue to impact people's lives positively in one way or another.

What are your guiding personal and business principles?

If I may list them; they are:

- ✓ Be humble
- ✓ Stay focused
- ✓ Listen actively to your customers
- ✓ Constantly innovate
- ✓ Stay at the top of your game
- ✓ Be excellent always in every single task you do

What is your greatest fear, and how do you manage fear?

Being alone - I am afraid of not having people around me one day. I am a very happy and social person, I always look for ways to widen my networks and meet new faces.

What is the best aspect of being an entrepreneur?

Deciding on the direction of my life and being in control of everything.

Do you have role models and why?
Not really.

What are your hobbies and what do you do to relax?

I have few of them which includes, swimming, listening to music, jogging and travelling

Do you have any favourite quote or saying?

Yes, I do: "If you can't fly then run, if you can't run then walk, if you can't walk then crawl, but whatever you do, you have to keep moving forward." - Martin Luther King

What advice or message do you have for young Africans who want to become entrepreneurs?

First, don't be afraid of risks and failures - remember the best time you have to be an entrepreneur is in your young age because you have all the time and life ahead. Africa needs you to solve its issues, your community needs you to help them - find your mission, find your passion and no matter how small you start, JUST START! Second, be passion driven - money will follow.

Great leaders are almost always great simplifiers, who cut through argument, debate and doubt to offer a solution everybody can understand and remember.

- Michael Korda

DOUG HOERNLE
Rethink Education

Doug Hoernle, a South African education technology entrepreneur is the Founder and Chief Executive Officer of Rethink Education.

Hoernle is passionate about improving Africa's future using innovative mobile technology. He has built a number of successful technology businesses, and Rethink Education has helped over half a million of students across Africa access premium Maths and Science content on their mobile devices.

Rethink Education has built and developed innovative mobile learning platforms, as well as the complete Grade 8 - 12 Maths and Science curriculum in an interface designed for mobile phones. Over 500,000 South African students are learning on the Rethink feature phone platform. It has worked and currently works with a number of established clients and various non-profit organisations and schools across South Africa.

The Interview:

How did the idea for your business come about?

Compared to 76 countries, South Africa's school children rank second to last in the world in mathematics, according to the most recent education report released by the Organisation for Economic Co-operation and Development (OECD) - beating only Ghana.

Recent matric results further highlighted the desperate state of maths teaching in the country when only a small minority of students passed the final examinations. Good quality maths and science teachers are in short supply and thousands of students (in rural areas in particular) don't have access to effective learning material.

I founded Rethink Education with a vision to make a significance difference in solving this problem by providing a mobile solution that provides access to quality maths and science learning material to students in both urban and rural areas who do not have access to basic learning material, extra maths classes or just qualified teachers.

Besides solving the access issue, the ultimate aim is to improve the maths and science literacy in the country and South Africa's ranking in the world. I fully believe that a bold intervention like this can go a long way in solving this problem in the country.

Give the readers some insight into your business?

Rethink Education has been building mathematics and science learning content for mobile phones since 2012 and deployed an application hosted on the instant messaging service, Mxit in 2012. At that stage Mxit was the largest mobile social network among South African students and our offering saw an uptake with more than 500,000 users actively interacting with the application on feature phones. In 2013, Rethink completed a usage study, in partnership with the Douglas Murray Trust, which, apart from convincing us of the potential for mobile learning, highlighted the need for teacher involvement, tracking of progress and gamification.

Recognising the uptake of smart-phones in the country, we rebuilt our mobile learning platform. Valuable lessons learnt from our usage study, resulted in the platform functionality being extended to include a teacher dashboard (to track performance and student engagement), and gamification (leader boards and incentives/rewards). The rethought platform and content was launched in July 2015 and since then we have been working with education foundations to implement a flipped classroom model alongside the formal schooling system.

In your opinion, what do you consider as some of the top skills needed to be a successful entrepreneur?

Passion, zest and grit!

What demographic group would you consider as your key clients?

Any person between the ages of 14 and 21 with access to a mobile phone and a willingness to improve their mathematics and science knowledge.

What have been some of your challenges and lessons learned from them?

I started my first business at the age of sixteen, and have learnt many things since then. There have been many challenges in all the businesses I have started. These ranges from raising funding, employing staff, managing teams, creating new business models, understanding technology, innovating as fast as possible and always trying to keep my head above the water. I have learnt to move at a breakneck pace and always be ready for the next opportunity and challenge thrown at me.

In today's challenging world, what do you do to stay on top of the game?

I read… I try to read as many biographies about great business leaders as possible. I think one can learn a huge amount from other successful business leaders, so I try and take lessons that I read about and apply them within my own businesses. I like to read biographies, especially about successful entrepreneurs. I learnt a lot by reading books on Warren Buffet, Steve Jobs, Jack Ma, Elon Musk etc, but find as much value reading about people who are successful in other fields, such as Scott Jurek, one of the world's most famous ultra marathon runners.

I am also a strong believer in mentorship and surround myself with people who are constantly challenging me to achieve at the best of my ability.

What does success mean to you and the best way to achieve long-term success?

I want to change the world… Simple!

What has been your most satisfying moment in business?

Seeing thousands of students in rural communities in Africa telling me the reason they excelled in Maths was due to their mobile phone and our application.

How has being an entrepreneur affected your (family) life?

I am incredibly lucky to have a very supportive family who have always been there in the tough times and celebrated with me during the good times. I am also lucky to have an amazing girl (now my fiancé) by my side, who as a high school teacher in an under-resourced school helps me understand the issues African students face on a daily basis.

What other sacrifices have you made to be a successful entrepreneur?

I have certainly sacrificed almost every weekend and holiday over the past few years. Innovating and growing a business required every bit of your time and ability. These sacrifices have been worth every single minute for seeing the impact we have had with our various tools.

On average, how many hours do you work per day and what is your typical day like?

I have never measured, however my typical day starts at 6am with an hour of exercise, either a run, in the gym or Pilates and yoga. I am normally in the office by around 7h15 and will be fighting fires until around 10pm. I get to travel a lot, so have learnt to work anywhere from an overnight plane trip to Dubai to a rural community in Limpopo in South Africa with very limited internet connectivity…

Where do you see yourself and business in another 10 years?

I am absolutely convinced by the power of mobile technology to create massive systemic change in Africa over the next ten years. I have positioned our business to be a leader in mobile technology and hope that we will grow to be able to influence and improve people's educations globally using their mobile device.

What are your guiding personal and business principles?

Honesty and punctuality! In the last fifteen years, I have NEVER been late for one appointment or meeting…. I also believe in loyalty and trust. I will do everything I can to live up to promises I make; however those promises often end up being far more challenging than I imagined up front.

What is your greatest fear, and how do you manage fear?

Being unable to pay my staff's salaries ;)

What is your best aspect of being an entrepreneur?

I am kept on my toes every single day. I cannot remember the last time I knew what I was going to be doing/where I was going to be the following week. That is extremely stimulating and incredibly challenging.

Do you have role models and why?

Most certainly, I look up to other successful entrepreneurs, as well as my peers who are innovating on a global scale and have more energy than I can imagine!

What are your hobbies and what do you do to relax?

I am a huge appreciator of fine wine and have an internationally accredited diploma in wine. I lecture certificate and diploma courses in wine and will never turn down a bottle of Burgundy, Bordeaux or perhaps a sweet wine from Hungary or German Riesling...

Do you have any favourite quote or saying?

"Life is like a snowball. The important thing is finding wet snow and a really long hill." - Warren Buffett.

What advice or message do you have for young Africans who want to become entrepreneurs?

Take every opportunity you can... You never know where the next big idea may be hiding!

One of the greatest regrets in life is being what others would want you to be rather than being yourself.

- Shannon Alder, Writer

ELIE KUAME
Elie Kuame Paris

Elie Kuame is the Fashion Creative & Artistic Director of Elie Kuame Paris, a fashion design label combining haute couture with prêt-á-porter.

Elie Kuame who has a unique heritage spanning four countries of Cote d'Ivoire, Mali, Mauritania and Lebanon started his fashion couture in 2006. Since then, he has designed and crafted stunning attires in France, Saudi Arabia, Lebanon, China, West Indies and across the continent of Africa.

The Interview:

How did the idea for your business come about?

Women have always impressed me in my family and particularly their strong sense of refinement. Therefore, I decided to pay tribute to my mother by celebrating all women. However, what really motivated me was when I moved to France to pursue my studies in Economics and Social Sciences, and I realised that Europeans had a completely inaccurate vision of Africa and therefore of us, Africans. For that reason, I decided to show, through my humble vision, how rich and noble our culture is.

Give the readers some insight into your business?

There are five of us in the team and we work with three haute couture seamstresses. We have two sections - one for ready wear and the other for Couture. Our showroom is located in Bastille, in the heart of Paris. Our work does a subtle bridge between Africa, the Middle East and the West so as to sublimate the feminine body using the precepts of tradition and the secrets of elegance. In 2010, Elie Kuame Paris was restructured and now composed of three ranges: Couture: Wedding dresses, Ball dresses.

By combining the love of silky and voluptuous materials with the originality and the nobility of African materials sublimated by delicate handmade middle-eastern embroidery, the Elie Kuame Paris House is the reflection of the cultural mosaic I have always been a part of. Influenced by the visual, emotional and conceptual elements found in the architecture, history, painting, travel and photography, arts, Elie Kuame operates the world around him with passion, attention and opportunism.

In your opinion, what do you consider as some of the top skills needed to be a successful entrepreneur?

To be a good entrepreneur, the key to success is to be passionate about what you have decided to fight for. You then need to arm yourself with determination, tenacity, humility and ambition.

What demographic group would you consider as your key clients?

Each woman who loves elegance, refinement, sophistication, comfort and luxury is a potential client for Elie Kuame Paris. For that reason, we have created a universe around women called "Women of Power".

What have been some of your challenges and lessons learned from them?

When you decide to become an entrepreneur, each day becomes a challenge. And when you live in France it is ten times harder. When I succeeded in presenting our SS16 collection, Hyper-Femme, at the same time as the Paris Fashion Week, I realised that nothing was impossible. Although I have made mistakes in the past but thanks to my Lord Jehovah, I have arisen and my business is working.

In today's challenging world, what do you do to stay on top of the game?

My watchword is a simple equation: Excellence and Rigour are equal to Elie Kuame Paris. We have transformed this equation into a lifestyle. Our challenge is growth.

What does success mean to you and the best way to achieve long-term success?

We will reach success when we give others the opportunity to valorise their ambitions through merit. In fact, we would like to open a production unit in Africa with a formative division. When they are ready, we would like the trainees to join the production unit. For that particular reason, we are currently actively seeking the investment this project requires. This is exactly why we need to develop our ready-to-wear line so that it is available on the global scene.

What has been your most satisfying moment in business?

Many moments: when I had the opportunity, through Hapsatou Sy, to settle in Central Paris and to start selling my ready-to-wear line; when I presented my collection on the fringe of the Paris Fashion week. I felt a great satisfaction. It was short but it made me understand all the things that were left to achieve and that we could succeed.

How has being an entrepreneur affected your (family) life?

To reach my goals, I refuse to compromise. This has led me to choose between my private life and my professional life, which I ended up giving more importance. I am totally devoted to my work so that I never lose sight of my aims. However I hope to settle down soon.

What other sacrifices have you made to be a successful entrepreneur?

Elie Kuame Paris has a golden rule: never refuse to satisfy a client, whatever the time, the delay, the complexity of her desire. Finding how to satisfy my clients is one of my greatest ability. I am therefore always available. Working with French dressmakers implies higher costs. We had to reduce our profit margin to maintain affordable prices.

On average, how many hours do you work per day and what is your typical day like?

When you are building an empire, work hours cannot be counted. The longest I have worked for was 8 days without sleeping. But it was because I had to!

Where do you see yourself and business in another 10 years?

I see myself: In my sewing room/office/lab sorting out dresses for awards like the Grammy's or the Oscars; managing the production for our corners at Bergoff Gudman, Nordstrom, Simmons, Barneys, Ostoura

Kuwait, etc; delivering orders in Nigeria, South Africa or even Shanghai; organising our training periods with our partners; providing enough data to our different branches in the world to lead our foundation destined to Women and Education.

What are your guiding personal and business principles?

In addition to cultural values my parents have given me, such as respect, availability and the taste for well-done work, my Bible is the most valuable thing to me. It allows me to never lose my head, whatever the circumstances. Humility, excellence, honesty, responsibility and a job well done are the qualities that dictate not only my professional life but also my private life. I am naturally unsatisfied and I always want to do better and go beyond my limits.

What is your greatest fear, and how do you manage fear?

My biggest fear is to lose my faith. It would shake my whole universe. The pure atmosphere that surrounds me as well as the clear vision of my future and the means to get there would be disturbed. This is the reason why I do not let anything disturb my line of conduct and my judgments, whatever the cost.

What is your best aspect of being an entrepreneur?

Each day is a new day. Each day is another chance to do well, to do better, to learn, to give hope, to receive, to smile, to create happiness, to fight, to repair your mistakes and most importantly to succeed.

Do you have role models and why?

My role models are Balmain and Elie Saab. With the right means and hard work, one has succeeded into reinventing itself and becoming a key player and the second to create desire and addiction. Nowadays, they both are worth millions of dollars and cannot be ignored when it comes to the international fashion scene. I call it excellence!

What are your hobbies and what do you do to relax?
I enjoy cooking, travelling, wine-tasting or even visiting museums. What relaxes me the most is being in Africa, my land, the land of my youth, my home.

Do you have any favourite quote or saying?

"Only hard work pays off."

What advice or message do you have for young Africans who want to become entrepreneurs?

Nowadays it is a necessity to always aim higher to reach our objectives. We have the duty of being hard working because only merit precedes success.

It is impossible to indulge in the silence of mediocrity excused by self-flagellation because we are the future. We therefore have the duty of doing everything so that the small seeds we've sown become tall baobabs, which will become a support to future generations. And we will succeed.

I have become my own version of an optimist. If I can't make it through one door, I'll go through another door, or I'll make a door. Something terrific will come no matter how dark the present.

- Rabindranath Tagore, Indian writer

EMEKA AKANO
Jara Mobile Limited

Emeka Akano is the co-founder and Chief Executive Officer of Jara Mobile Limited, a start-up mobile commerce platform that disrupts the way people think about purchasing airtime and paying bills. Its flagship product *Jara App* rewards users with cash back in the form of discount coupons to top brand outlets every time they buy airtime or pay bills.

Mr Akano, an Electrical and Electronics Engineer by training has worked in the roles of an IT Engineer,

Research Engineer, Project Manager, and also as a Business Development Executive across the Oil and Gas sector, Government, Manufacturing sector and Educational sector.

The Interview:

How did the idea for your business come about?

The idea came after I stumbled on a survey released by National Bureau of Statistics (NBS) done in collaboration with the World Bank which revealed that in the fiscal year of 2012/2013, Nigerians spent more talking on the telephone than they did on household items. When my co-founders and I did the math on the numbers, we discovered that the average airtime spent per active GSM subscriber was N3, 300 or $15 per month.

We saw how big a market the airtime recharge was and the fact that the numbers of registered lines were increasing each year in line with our population, we decided to go into the space to position ourselves for the future. Even though it was a crowded market, the bulk of the distribution of the product (airtime reselling) was done through paper scratch card, with less virtual. We knew that in few years, with the increase in smartphone penetration and internet penetration more of the payments of the bill would be done virtually and through the convenience of a mobile phone. We also had to think about how to differentiate ourselves because there were also few players in the market and we did not want to be just another player. We wanted to give consumers more value by partnering with retail brands that were looking for more effective ways to reach and engage consumers. That was how Jara was born. Jara in the Nigeria local language means giving extra value!

Give the readers some insight into your business?

Consumers use our app to make routine payments like airtime purchase and for each transaction they get rewarded instantly with discount coupon(s) for their transaction to top quality brands, enabling them to save on their routine lifestyle activities. While brands innovatively acquire new customers, market to targeted consumers and gain consumer insights, leading to a win-win-win business model for both consumers and brands.

In your opinion, what do you consider as some of the top skills needed to be a successful entrepreneur?

Some of the top skills are: determination, the ability to be persistent, the ability to be dynamic, focused and leadership skills.

What demographic group would you consider as your key clients?

Young, tech savvy and trendy people between the age of 18 and 40 are our key clients. Further broken into two segments, our class A customers are 25-40 young professionals who are also trendy and tech savvy and the class B customers are the 18-25 year olds who are students.

What have been some of your challenges and lessons learned from them?

Accessing funds and business capital in Nigeria is a challenge. Getting quality human resources is another, especially in my field where software development is at the core of product development. For fund raising, you have to be extra determined and focused to attract capital as people would hardly give you money from only doing a PowerPoint presentation on an idea. Your self-belief in bootstrapping to do all that is required by building the first set of prototypes, official business registrations and setups plus other assessments like integrity or competence or ability to execute are required to convince the investors or supporters come into play. This approach is also applicable to attracting quality human resources which you may not be able to afford at the early stages of your venture. When people see your focus, determination and belief, which takes time to prove, they are more compelled to help you out at the early days which are critical before your business grows to a point where you can compete or pay for their services.

In today's challenging world, what do you do to stay on top of the game?

I try to acquire new knowledge and skills as often as possible, as the saying goes that "information is power." I truly believe in it and try to get as much information as I can to stay on top of the game.

What does success mean to you and the best way to achieve long-term success?

Success for me, is doing what you love doing and fulfilling your purpose here on earth. The best way to achieve long term success is through hard-work and dedication in pursuing one's goals and by going at it with integrity at all times.

What has been your most satisfying moment in business?

When a new person is employed and guaranteed to earn a decent wage or salary from the job that I have been able to create from my engagement in business.

How has being an entrepreneur affected your (family) life?

I would say the pressure got to my immediate family especially in the early days. I thank God for the privilege of having had a good education, thanks to my parents - they are simply the best! They were not entirely sure about my career move as they had hoped I'd stay in a paid employment much longer before setting out to start a business due to the acclaimed job security of being in paid employment. I'm not yet married which may also be largely due to the fact that I have been nurturing my business venture which is time consuming at the early stages.

What other sacrifices have you made to be a successful entrepreneur?

I have had to sacrifice my comfort and quality of living

in order to use my savings to bootstrap my business ventures. When I decided to relocate back to Nigeria from England where I was based, I pretty much sold off most of my electronics and household items, and plunged the money into the venture I was working on at the time, which did not even take off. Among others, I also ate lesser meals every day for several months as part of bootstrapping.

On average, how many hours do you work per day and what is your typical day like?

I work an average of 11 to 13 hours daily on week days on business related activities. On weekends, it drops a bit due to other personal engagements like weddings, church etc, but we usually have meetings with Advisors for strategy and advisory sessions on most weekends. From 7am when I wake up, I start responding to work emails and related messages over social messenger applications or make phone calls. I do these after my "quiet time" where I read my Bible and pray or do some reading of whatever book I am reading at the time. I am still working on having a steady exercise routine to be done after my quiet time. Once I get on my workstation, I draft out the items I want tackled for the day if I did not already do that the night before and make a note of their priorities and then I start navigating through the day as dynamically as possible to achieve a productive day. At the end of the day I review what I was able to achieve which influences my strategy for the next day.

Where do you see yourself and business in another 10 years?

My overall entrepreneurial vision in life is to set up different businesses across several industries which would help reduce the high rate of unemployment in Nigeria and Africa. In ten years however, I see myself diversifying the business portfolio of *Jara Mobile Limited* with more service offerings relevant to the market while also having ventured into a different business sectors other than the

IT/ICT/internet sector. It may well still be a 'software as a service' business model for another sector, because I am a strong believer in the use of technology to make life a bit easier and more enjoyable. In summary, I see myself being a thought business leader who would have created a lot of jobs for Africans.

What are your guiding personal and business principles?

Integrity, reliability, respect and fairness!

What is your greatest fear, and how do you manage fear?

I am not entirely sure if I have any greatest fear. However I do like the feeling of "You did not get that right" or "making mistakes", but I manage it by reminding myself that whenever I do not get it right or I get the decision wrong, I have actually gotten a bit more information of how I would get it right the next time or how I should make the decision another time and that is not the end of the world.

What is your best aspect of being an entrepreneur?

The bit where I get to impact society directly be it in job creation for individuals who would not have had a job or the value being created in the economy as a whole. I also enjoy the flexibility of working on my own terms.

Do you have role models and why?

I do have role models across different fields and works of life and I have them because they are real life examples which showcase possibilities in achieving excellence across different things and aspects of business and life in general. A role model for public speaking, another for business venture creation and so on. Role models are people who are already doing either exactly what I am aspiring to do or a bit of it; they help me reckon with the possibilities of achieving.

What are your hobbies and what do you do to relax?

I like dancing and listening to music, playing football, watching football as well as playing snooker.

Do you have any favourite quote or saying?

"Anything worth doing is worth doing well".

What advice or message do you have for young Africans who want to become entrepreneurs?

Budding young African entrepreneurs should seek knowledge relevant to entrepreneurship and how to start and manage a business. I understand many schools around the world including African schools do not have entrepreneurial modules being taught in the curriculum, so with this, budding entrepreneurs come out of school without any knowledge of what it takes to start or even run a successful business. Secondly, they should know their strengths and weaknesses. For example, it is important to know that he/she lacks interpersonal skills, because this would enable them to identify the type of partners to have on board to compliment them. Entrepreneur cannot go far without the right team members or partners when trying to solve a problem or execute an idea.

We should all open our eyes and minds to the limitless possibilities the world has to offer.

- Lisa Messenger

EMO RUGENE
Nyala Sneaker Collection

The Nyala collection is an embodiment of intercity and multi-culturally inspired footwear that cuts across three capital cities.

The Nyala Sneaker is designed in Berlin, Germany and inspired by the architecture of its massive buildings, long visual axes, high ceilings and beauty that is inconspicuous. The sneaker collection is also influenced by the vibrancy and eclectic nature of Nairobi, Kenya where the designer, Emo Rugene, grew up and it is produced in Addis Ababa, "The New Flower".

Nyala is an Amharic word meaning Gazelle, a tribute to the beauty, elegance and agility of this animal, which was a central part of the design process.

Emo Rugene who holds a BA in International Relations from Kenya and an M,A. in Peace Studies from Austria, is an Actor, Model and designer Entrepreneur behind Nyala Collections.

After his promising career as a footballer was cut short by injuries, he decided to pursue his second passion in fashion. He started out as a stylist for a major African fashion house, working on numerous fashion events, music videos and photo shoots for both corporate clients and individuals. He later veered into modelling where he graced numerous runways and fashion Editorial spreads.

Each piece in the collection uses beautiful African fabrics, including sheep leather, textiles sourced from Kenya.

Nyala Collections which have been featured in the KLM travel magazine are currently stocked in various outlets across the world.

The Interview:

How did the idea for your business come about?

I started my business in 2012 where at the time I was a model and realised that there is a gap in the design industry in Kenya because there was no brand making shoes at the time and this is why I decided to start my own company.

Give the readers some insight into your business?

The Nyala Collections brands also called Afro Shoes are designer footwears which incorporate African fabric that gives it the aesthetic look.

In your opinion, what do you consider as some of the top skills needed to be a successful entrepreneur?

I think persistence and drive is key, because as an entrepreneur there are a lot of situations where one will be called upon to push through; failure is part of being a successful Businessperson and this is what makes one successful. Falling and getting back up.

What demographic group would you consider as your key clients?

I honestly think that my target market is anyone with feet. With time however, I have realised that most of my clientele are people who want to have an edge in their outfits and my shoes definitely bring that.

What have been some of your challenges and lessons learned from them?

I have learnt that the customer is key to the success of the business and if you treat the client right, they will refer you and this is how you grow. I have dealt with clients on all levels in Kenya and it is all the same. If you respect them you get a better response.

Some business people become arrogant and this is where they lose the client base.

In today's challenging world, what do you do to stay on top of the game?

By reading a lot! There is a lot to still learn and room to get better. The best way I find to do this is learning from those who have been there before you.

What does success mean to you and the best way to achieve long-term success?

Success to me is achieving and surpassing set targets. Keeping an eye on the ball and it's hard work that can only do this. For me, there is no substitute for hard work.

What has been your most satisfying moment in business?

It changes because I have been setting targets and achieving them. At the moment I can say it's being able to do two successful crowd-funding projects both in Kenya and Germany.

How has being an entrepreneur affected your (family) life?

I have never known anything else than being an entrepreneur; so it is not a change that we have had to adjust to as a family. Though I understand that being in charge of one's business is a full time job where I find myself thinking about business even on holiday.

What other sacrifices have you made to be a successful entrepreneur?

A hard decision that I had to make was to part ways with my initial hard workers that I made shoes with before I set up my own workshop.

On average, how many hours do you work per day and what is your typical day like?

I work many hours per day which involves being a lot on the road, phone calls, emails and correspondence on social media. I wake up to reply to pending messages, check in at the workshop, plan for the inventory for the day, go to the gym and then have meetings or interviews in the afternoons.

Where do you see yourself and business in another 10 years?

I see myself as an influencer in African fashion and also hope to open up a big workspace that can be a training centre for upcoming designers and in this space we can be able to produce brands in the continent for the world market.

What are your guiding personal and business principles?

I believe in honesty and transparency. These two have guided me from the start and the results are out there for all to see.

What is your greatest fear, and how do you manage fear?

My biggest fear is being broke and this at the moment is keeping me at bay by working hard and doing my best in whatever I do.

What is your best aspect of being an entrepreneur?

It's the buying and selling. It's the negotiations and the wits that you need in business. This does it for me.

Do you have role models and why?

My role model is my mum. She managed as a single mother to raise my sister and I to be confident self-standing human beings, all this while she worked long hours.

What are your hobbies and what do you do to relax?

I do a lot of sports. I almost played professional football so I workout almost every day; be it at the gym, boxing or playing football.

Do you have any favourite quote or saying?

You live and you learn. I believe we all learn from the experiences we go through and I prefer to look at the positive side of it than the negative side.

What advice or message do you have for young Africans who want to become entrepreneurs?

I would say that if you want to be an entrepreneur go for it but keep in mind that it is a hard road ahead with challenges that only serve to test your resolve and these will make you question yourself and how much you want it but you know what, It is totally worth it at the end of it!

To avoid criticism, do nothing, say nothing, be nothing.

- Elbert Hubbard

ERIC KACOU
ESPartners

Eric Kacou who was raised in Cote d'Ivoire co-founded Entrepreneurial Solutions Partners (ESPartners) of which he's the current Chief Executive Officer.

After a career as a business strategy adviser, Eric Kacou became convinced that entrepreneurs are the best actors to create jobs, wealth and prosperity through their products and services.

ESPartners whose mission is to deploy Intelligent Capital, the right combination of

Insights & Investments to enable growth of high- impact entrepreneurs, gave the reason why it exist as the "Believe in the power of entrepreneurs to enable prosperity. Yet, entrepreneurs in Africa face a vicious cycle keeping their businesses under skilled, undercapitalized and vulnerable. We exist to help these entrepreneurs grow."

ESPartners want to achieve its goals through these three prong approach:

Incubate Ventures - running a variety of entrepreneurial competition and supporting incubators and accelerators to enable early stage development; **Generating Insights** - working directly with firms as a strategic advisor to help them grow their business; and **High Impact Ventures** - facilitating capital raises and investing directly in high impact ventures.

The Interview:

How did the idea for your business come about?

In 2010, after some 15 years working with leaders in Africa and beyond, I realised that progress towards prosperity was not uniform. For every country with tremendous growth - such as Rwanda, where I have been honoured to work and witness real transformation, there are many more that have struggled or stumbled after growth.

I started to think about the real drivers of sustainable economic growth. This journey led me to write my book as a way to share the ideas and solutions that I observed. I decided to go beyond the book by starting a business, a platform to deliver some of my proposed solutions to African leaders and entrepreneurs; and ESPartners was born.

Give the readers some insight into your business?

ESPartners is all about people. We are entrepreneurs serving entrepreneurs and leaders with a high-impact potential. We are a team of professionals of different backgrounds and cultures but sharing the same purpose, desire and vision to transform Africa. We all are innovative entrepreneurs, willing to make a difference. ESPartners are also the leaders we are proud and fortunate to work with.

In a nutshell, ESPartners is a strategy consulting and investment boutique providing high-potential entrepreneurs and leaders with the right mix of insight and capital needed to address the challenges facing African economies and to translate the continent's potential into prosperity.

To achieve our vision, we design solution-oriented strategies and tools, adapted to our environment in many parts of Africa. Our organisation is structured into three key ways.

The first is incubating businesses, we implement high-impact and customized incubation and acceleration programme as well as entrepreneurial competitions in support of early stage ventures.

The second is through our insights generation. This includes serving as strategic advisors to both businesses in the growth phase and to other private sector enabling stakeholders to improve ecosystems and private sector led development.

Lastly, we invest in high potential entrepreneurs through our investment arm - ESP Capital - a fund designed to provide the right mix of capital and insights to francophone West Africa's missing middle with regional and pan African growth potential. We are currently fundraising for this vehicle and are hoping to have our first close soon.

In 2013, we launched the first chapter of ESPartners not-for profit entrepreneurial platform - Archimedean & Entrepreneurs (A&E) - in Cote d'Ivoire. Our ambition is now to scale up the platform in Cote d'Ivoire as well as in francophone West Africa and to bring A&E to Rwanda.

In your opinion, what do you consider as some of the top skills needed to be a successful entrepreneur?

Six years into my business, every day offers countless learning opportunities. Actually, I have learnt a lot from entrepreneurs who have been and still are my mentors. I suspect that I will never cease to learn.

Building on my experience, I would say that the first skill to have is listening. A good entrepreneur dedicates time and cares to listen to others; it requires humility to listen rightly and not being defensive, and attention to clearly identify people's needs and ideas and wishes.

The second quality is adaptability. In a constantly changing world, one must be able to reinvent oneself and learn from those changes. This is particularly true in Africa and the rest of the developing world where entrepreneurs face a myriad of additional challenges.

Finally, I would say that ambition is essential. It enables one to listen to one's own vision, without being led by others' guidelines and fears. And this is paramount when you are an entrepreneur. Similarly, I believe entrepreneurs must have a good measure of tenacity and resilience.

What demographic group would you consider as your key clients?

Most of our beneficiaries are young people between 19 and 35. We work all over the African continent and across sectors but we rather focus on underserved African markets including franco-phone and luso-phone countries. We have regional offices in Cote d'Ivoire, Rwanda and a presence in Angola.

Beyond demographics, what matters most is the mindset of the people we work with. The common denominator among all our partners is their vision. We are fortunate to work with leaders and entrepreneurs of all age, gender and country who challenge the status quo and are open to innovation.

What have been some of your challenges and lessons learned from them?

The first main challenge is to expand and scale up our business and impact. We have been able to build and run successful programmes for up to a couple thousand entrepreneurs at a time but we are still far from our goal of one million entrepreneurs! This is a tremendous but exciting challenge.

The second challenge is to measure impact. To be fully accountable and to assess how our action improves the ecosystem, we still have to develop a rigorous M&E system. That is why a key lesson we learnt from entrepreneurs is how incorporating technology into our work to be more impactful and innovative. This is a great piece we are working on.

What does success mean to you and the best way to achieve long-term success?

Success to me means having a demonstrable impact on people's life. On the long term, it is to give the opportunity to anyone we work with to grow and develop their full potential.

What has been your most satisfying moment in business?

It is very satisfying to acknowledge that things are going by themselves without my personal involvement. When the machine is running without you, it is actually very fulfilling! And it happens more and more often at ESPartners! Recently, I was very fortunate to attend the launch of the new promotion of our entrepreneurial platform A&E that my team successfully organised - and where I was not involved beyond leading a training session!
That being said, seeing the entrepreneurs we support achieving their goals and growing thriving, prosperous businesses is always gratifying. It was rewarding to see many Ivorian entrepreneurs we have supported among the 35

innovators under 35 to watch in French-speaking countries.

How has being an entrepreneur affected your (family) life?

It is very tough indeed. Being an entrepreneur led me to start this part of my life tardily and till now, my entrepreneurial activities may be at the expense of my family life.

Where do you see yourself and business in another 10 years?

In another 10 years, I hope that my team and I would have impacted 1 million entrepreneurs across our continent and have inspired others to do the same.

It's difficult to pursue a dream. It's a tragedy not to.

- Oprah Winfrey

ERIC KINOTI
Shades System East Africa

32-year-old Eric Kinoti is the Founder and Director of Shade Group Limited, the umbrella parent of 5 companies.

Shade Systems (EA) Limited is a tent manufacturing company and Installer of all types of shade solutions. His other companies are: Alma Tents Limited, sound and events' requirement hiring company; Bag Base Kenya Limited, a manufacturer of all type of bags; SafiSana Home Services Limited, a professional home cleaning company and Entrepreneurs Boot Camp Limited, an annual event that brings together entrepreneurs, business leaders and investors.

Kinoti's success has won him several accolades over the years. He has been listed in Kenya's Top 40 under 40 and Forbes Top 30 under 30 and voted the Most Influential SME personality at the SOMA Awards.

The Interview:

How did the idea for your business come about?

I was doing school supplies in Western Kenya and one day I met someone who wanted a tent. I said I can get the tent. I came back to Nairobi and did my research and I found out that not so many people made tents and those who did imported materials from China. As I continued to do my research, it became clearer that there was a gap in tents making in Kenya. That's how Shade Systems was born. Other companies were demand driven.

Give the readers some insight into your business?

Shade Systems Kenya is the premier provider of shade solutions under the sun. We manufacture and custom build restaurant canopies, marquees, swimming pool shades, canopy tents, lorry tarpaulins, garden umbrellas, wheel covers, branded gazebos, bouncing castles, school bags and a wide range of other customized products.

Shade Systems Kenya has established itself as the undisputed leader in manufacture of tents for sale in Kenya and with extensive experience it has been able to progress and achieve increased targets every year. We are a trusted & reliable name, associated for a long time now with tents and tarpaulins because of excellence in producing finest quality products.

In your opinion, what do you consider as some of the top skills needed to be a successful entrepreneur?

You need great leadership qualities. There is a very thin line between leadership and entrepreneurship, but they go hand in hand. You also need to be very focused and keep to details. Being keen to details and everything happen around you is a skill that you acquire with time and experience.

What demographic group would you consider as your key clients?

We cater for every demographic but some of our products best suits the high-end people; those that are looking to maintain a status quo and leave a luxury life.

What have been some of your challenges and lessons learned from them?

When I started, I had challenges in guidance. Being a very young and naïve ambitious man, I got into some issues that could be avoided only if I had mentorship. This is something some very many young entrepreneurs are struggling with. As a result of this, I vowed when I make it, I will give back to the young by doing as much mentorship as I could. Right now I have an annual event called Entrepreneurs Boot Camp, a three-day event that we mentor; shape and help young entrepreneurs get funds and partnerships. I also mentor young people through talks and my social media platforms.

I learnt that mentorship is one of the most important steps you can take to lay a foundation for success. When you have expert guidance, support, and motivation, you are 100 times more unstoppable than when you are alone. Mentorship allows you to quantum leap straight to the head of the game more rapidly than if you tediously faced down every beginner's hurdle.

In today's challenging world, what do you do to stay on top of the game?

I am a very prayerful person. I wake up early to have time with God. I seek guidance, knowledge and wisdom. I also have a very creative team that I work with. We try to always be a step forward in everything we do. Innovation and strategy is key!

What does success mean to you and the best way to achieve long-term success?

Success means a lot of things to different people. To me, success is being able to accomplish every day's target and going to bed with my to-do list done. By this, I mean being able to provide solutions and improving the quality of life is a big success to me. To achieve long term success, you have got to remain very focused, work smart and treat money as a secondary factor to your business. If you make money your primary factor or reason to being in business, then you wouldn't achieve much.

What has been your most satisfying moment in business?

Being able to serve international clients.

How has being an entrepreneur affected your (family) life?

It has affected me positively. I have gained great and powerful networks that are very crucial in any industry. I have learned to manage my time and schedules; that way there is no aspect of my life that I neglect.

What other sacrifices have you made to be a successful entrepreneur?

I have lost friends, but I am very cool with that. The ups and downs of entrepreneurship makes you know your true friends; who are in for the ride and who are your-ride and die.

On average, how many hours do you work per day and what is your typical day like?

Uhm! I think I am actively working for 5 hours, then the rest of my day is more of networking and 'looking' for business deals. I wake up at 3:30 in the morning. I Say my prayer and get ready by 4:30. I am always in the office by 5:00 a.m. I do my work for three hours, and then do my business meeting for two hours. By 11:00 I am mostly out of the office.

Where do you see yourself and business in another 10 years?

In 10 years, I will have branches in at least 20 African countries; profit of 500 million annually and employing 1000 people and indirectly benefiting 1 million people.

What are your guiding personal and business principles?

Always Be Honest. There are no limits but we only limit ourselves.

What is your greatest fear, and how do you manage fear?

I have learnt how to face my fears. My biggest fear is that I am very ambitious but now I have learnt how to take calculated risks.

What is your best aspect of being an entrepreneur?

Working for myself and providing employment to more than 70 people/families.

Do you have role models and why?

I admire Dr. SK Macharia of Royal Media services. I believe that he has fought for his space and for his stations to be where they are today; sheer hard work and dedication has been put in.

What are your hobbies and what do you do to relax?

I like to network and meet new people.

Do you have any favourite quote or saying?

There are no permanent situations. Anyone can be whatever they want to be and achieve whatever; as long as they respect the process.

What advice or message do you have for young Africans who want to become entrepreneurs?

If you truly want to succeed, put in 100 percent effort. Effort will always trump luck and skill; so if you are serious about being an entrepreneur, then you should never stop trying.

Talent is cheaper than table salt. What separates the talented individual from the successful one is a lot of hard work.

- Stephen King

EUGENIE NYIRAMBONIGABA
Home Appetite Kigali

Eugenie Nyirambonigaba is the Founder of Home Appétit in Rwanda. She is the country's premier female head chef specializing in home catering for events and families of both Rwandese and expats.

This entrepreneur has over a decade of professional experience working as a chef. Her passion for food as well as her team's excellent customer service skills have led to recognition and high praise from clients.

Though known as Home Appétit, the company offer diverse services in bespoke cooking classes, private Chef Services, dinner parties & events, whole food diets and corporate affairs and catering.

Eugenie Nyirambonigaba: Muraho! That's how we say hello in Rwanda, in Kinyarwanda our national language.

The Interview:

How did the idea for your business come about?

I worked as housekeeper for many years, and wanted more than anything to become a real businesswoman. One day, someone asked me to share my dreams - this moment changed my life. I'd never been asked that before! I loved cooking and wanted more than anything to learn recipes from around the world and share them with others. So I enrolled in culinary school with the help of a sponsor. We noticed a gap in the market - many people in Rwanda have hired help to cook for their families, but there are no norms and standards to ensure quality, and food safety. My company provides this training to local staff. We also come to your home and cook for you, either with healthy meals for your family, or for a one-off event. Then the name was easy "Home Appetit!"

Give the readers some insight into your business?

The business is growing - and we have two objectives: (1) providing delicious and unique food to clients in Kigali, and (2) mentoring young girls to give them the skills needed to enter the culinary industry. We specialise in Asian food, as this is unique to Kigali and my favourite is Vietnamese! But we've learned recipes and styles from around the world. We specialise in focussing on healthy food, and apply nutrition principles to our work.

In your opinion, what do you consider as some of the top skills needed to be a successful entrepreneur?

Starting your own business is challenging, especially in a

country where entrepreneurial skills training is not always available. I've had to learn everything from the ground up, and there are some key skills your need. The most important are persistence and patience. Persistence because you can't know everything at once - it takes time to learn how to market yourself, how to speak to clients, how to get a website, how to get business cards. It also takes patience - I wanted everything at once. This is impossible. It's best to sit down and make a business plan - think about each element of your business and write it down. Make big goals, and then smaller goals. Lastly, build a team and be a leader - inspire others with your business goal and make them feel a part of it. Find people with skills in accounting/finance, and in web/communications. If you have faith, success will come.

What demographic group would you consider as your key clients?

We mainly provide services for international expats and professional Rwandans living in Kigali. Many work for international organisations, the United Nations, Government, banking and private sector industries.

What have been some of your challenges and lessons learned from them?

Finding enough time to do things is difficult. I do not have enough time to offer bespoke services, and also focus on growing the business. I need more people to help me succeed; reason why my husband joined my company - he works as a driver to make our services more effective. I'm saving to get a space with a bigger kitchen, but it really takes time. The challenge is knowing where to put my efforts to get the biggest rewards.

In today's challenging world, what do you do to stay on top of the game?

Rwanda is becoming a digital hub, and internet is the key to my success. This is where I advertise my business, meet new clients, showcase referrals and connect with the world.

Having a website and professional email is critical to my success. Using social media platforms like Instagram and Facebook has been key to connecting with others. I also want to learn more about the free Google services for managing my business. I'm also improving my English!

What does success mean to you and the best way to achieve long-term success?

To me, success is simply about meeting my two business objectives, but also being able to provide for my family, and to give my daughter the best life possible. I try to live by a mantra that we should all leave the world better than we found it. My family were all murdered in the genocide, so I live each day with their memory. Once I have a big kitchen and more staff, I'll know I've made it.

What has been your most satisfying moment in business?

I received a call from a potential client, who was referred to me by someone else. I was so happy with the word of mouth, and cooked for a Rwandan family, for over 50 people. It was my first big gig and I was so nervous. Everyone loved the food, and the client called me out to see the guests after the event. Everyone applauded. I have never been so proud.

How has being an entrepreneur affected your (family) life?

I'm the first female Head Chef in Rwanda. Due to the genocide, I was never able to finish school and thought I would be living in poverty for the rest of my life. Education changed everything for me - graduating from culinary school was the start of my future. My story inspires other women to work hard to achieve their dreams. My daughter's perspective on what is possible has changed, for the better. And my husband works for my company. Imagine! It has really brought us together, working towards a common goal.

What other sacrifices have you made to be a successful entrepreneur?

I work long hours, and this keeps me from my family sometimes. But I manage; everything is worth it as I know that each hour of work brings me one step closer to a better future.

On average, how many hours do you work per day and what is your typical day like?

I usually work about 10 hours a day. In the morning I go to a client's home, and cook for their family, or offer cooking classes. In the afternoon I usually go to a second client's home. Sometimes in the evenings, I work at catering events. I also have to fill in taking my daughter to school, checking emails and social media, and doing the accounts. On weekends, I mentor other girls in my home, and research recipes and menu plans for clients.

Where do you see yourself and business in another 10 years?

I'd love to have my own training centre for young people to come and gain culinary skills, and to offer cooking and nutrition classes to Rwandan families. I hope to step out of the actual cooking (except special events) and focus on business management. There is a long way to go, but I keep my persistence and patience.

What are your guiding personal and business principles?

Always remain courteous and professional. If a client is unhappy, ensure you understand why. Build trust in your services and yourself, but also, respect yourself. I am a professional and therefore charge a wage that matches my skills and experience. Often I have potential clients who do not respect this, asking to pay me less. Sometimes as an initial courtesy, I will offer a special, but I will not compromise myself just to get clients. Most of my clients respect that, and are happy with my services and rates. As long as you remain professional, the business keeps its integrity.

What is your greatest fear, and how do you manage fear?

My greatest fear is in disappointing my family. Everything I do, I do for them. I know they are proud of me, but I really want to show them that I am capable of reaching my goals. This fuels me to work harder each day. Sometimes the days are tough, but I think of how far I've come and recognise success - this gets me ahead.

What is your best aspect of being an entrepreneur?

Having the flexibility to choose the direction of the business. I am so proud of Home Appetit Kigali and all that I've achieved. I like being able to create a strategic vision.

Do you have role models and why?

Three years ago, I found a cookbook by Ms. Vy, a Vietnamese women entrepreneur. She came from nothing, and worked her way up through persistence and patience. She studied in France and now owns a number of restaurants and cooking schools in Vietnam. Her story was so inspiring and it taught me that dreams can come true. I think of her anytime I struggle. We've connected on Facebook, and one day I hope to meet her in person.

What are your hobbies and what do you do to relax?

I cook! It's funny, as it's my profession, but I love cooking at home for my family. I also go to Church; being close to God is so important to my family - He is responsible for blessing us with this life. Lastly, being with my daughter, Teta, is the most relaxing. There is nothing like coming home from a long day and having your child wrap their arms around you and tell you they love you. She is my everything!

Do you have any favourite quote or saying?

"She is clothed in strength and dignity and she laughs without fear of the future."

What advice or message do you have for young Africans who want to become entrepreneurs?

Don't be afraid to ask someone for help. Do research yourself - go to a local library or skills centre and read about entrepreneurship. Come up with a plan, and then go and ask for assistance. Look up "business networking events" in your city. Put on your best outfit, and show up. Never think "I don't belong there", or "they'll wonder why I'm here." People will be impressed. Instead of saying "can you help me?", you can turn up and say, "Hello my name is xxx. I am here to learn about business and entrepreneurship. I have a dream to run my own business one day. How did you achieve success?" Asking people about themselves and their experience will teach you so much, and eventually, the right person will recognise your talents. Don't give up!

People are not lazy. They simply have impotent goals - that is, goals that do not inspire them.

- Tony Robbins

GLORIA KAMANZI UWIZERA
Glo Creations

Gloria Kamanzi Uwizera is the Founder and Chief Executive Officer of Glo Creations, a textile design and home décor outfit in Rwanda.

She is behind the creative side of the company, working passionately on drawings, patterns and the hand printing techniques. She started the business at the age of 24 "with no clue of how my business future will look like."

The young female entrepreneur and designer was born in Brussels, the capital of Belgium, raised by Rwandan parents and lived in a number of African countries such as Kenya, Uganda, DR Congo and Senegal.

Gloria serves on the board of the Rwanda Fair Trade Artisan Association as its president representing the artisan's voices. She is also a member of a number of women entrepreneur's association such as Peace Through Business alumni, AWEP (a

U.S. State department programme).

The Interview:

How did the idea for your business come about?

The inspiration for starting my business was drawn from my grandfather and mother. As a small child, I was very passionate about drawing and colouring images, and in fact, I kept on developing my drawing skills until my teen-age. In 2004, while living in Senegal where I was pursuing my studies, my Aunt introduced me to a textile printing technique known as batik; then I realised that my drawing skill would match with the batik printing, I learnt the new skill of batik printing and decided to do it as a hobby. I started printing on t-shirts and have them sold at church on Sundays.

A few months later, as my small hobby was growing, I decided to turn it into a business profession and started thinking of returning to Rwanda. In 2005, I returned home with a vision of creating jobs and in 2006, I started my business despite the discouragement faced from a number of voices due to my young age and being a lady.

Give the readers some insight into your business?

Glo Creations is a Rwandan based textile design and printing company, specializing in creating African inspired quality patterns for garments and home interiors. Our work is to design, print on textile with hand techniques, then produce beautiful textile products. The major portion of the Glo Creations product range is textile-based and includes printed fabrics, ready-to-wear garments, home interior fabrics and products.

In your opinion, what do you consider as some of the top skills needed to be a successful entrepreneur?

For me, the top skills are: Knowing my vision, being fearless, ambitious, passionate, risk taking and having the ability to innovate.

What demographic group would you consider as your key clients?

My key clients are: Individuals of high and medium class, including the young and old. Our actual target is the young generation group and it's mostly composed of women from 20 to 50 years old.

What have been some of your challenges and lessons learned from them?

At the beginning, I didn't have the basics on business management. Other challenges faced were: access to funding, access to tailored trainings for specific industry such as the textile industry, access to coaching programmes. Despite all the challenges faced, I learnt to be focused on my dream and vision. Few years later, I joined a number of networks where I benefited from a number of programmes and connections which have contributed greatly to my business. I learnt from people's experiences on their entrepreneurial journey, and one thing that has kept me to pursue my entrepreneurial journey is passion for my work.

In today's challenging world, what do you do to stay on top of the game?

It's not always easy to stay on top as competition is becoming fierce globally but I would say with my experience, I have been working on my ability to innovate in order to explore opportunities.

What does success mean to you and the best way to achieve long-term success?

Success to me is making a difference in people's lives while doing what I'm passionate about. The best way to achieve long term success is to keep our credibility towards the people we serve.

What has been your most satisfying moment in business?

The most satisfying moment in my business was when I was giving a task by an international organisation together with the Rwanda government. The time to deliver was very short but with determination, I had to believe the impossible and not allow fear take over. It required me to be more confident and it also encouraged my team to be confident. At the end, the task was delivered on time. We learnt not to underestimate ourselves as a team.

How has being an entrepreneur affected your (family) life?

My entrepreneurial life has affected my family life so much that I rarely attend family gatherings. My business has its unexpected season or moment where I would hardly avail myself for important family matters.

What other sacrifices have you made to be a successful entrepreneur?

A lot of sacrifices have been made, such as not taking holidays. I have had to reduce my leisure time. As the business goes through its growth, it's time consuming and must fill some gaps to make sure the operation moves on.

On average, how many hours do you work per day and what is your typical day like?

My days are quite busy with usually 10 to 12 work hours. I start each work day in the workshop with my employees reviewing the work tasks, then make appointments with the clients in the afternoon. Each day is different from another, as I undertake a number of few occupations within the organisation.

Where do you see yourself and business in another 10 years?

I see myself among the top Textile designers on the African continent. The company's vision is to be the leading textile design company in Rwanda, in the next few years. We are also looking at setting up a new modern production facility for larger production and have a number of stores on the African continent.

What are your guiding personal and business principles?

Practice the art of self control, creativity, persistence and passion. I am the kind of person who does things with details and precision.

What is your greatest fear, and how do you manage fear?

My greatest fear is to disappoint and fail on a task or assignment.

What is your best aspect of being an entrepreneur?

Creating opportunities; making a difference in the process and standing up for what I believe in.

Do you have role models and why?

Armi Ratia, the founder of Marimekko. Armi envisioned a bold future for textile design and manufacturing. Marimekko is one of the top textile design brand in Finland, Europe and globally. Armi, as a female designer and entrepreneur, has changed the Finnish fashion by promoting the hand printed cotton fabrics. Armi has been an inspirational reference to my career as I pursue my journey in the textile design industry and she has been a role model even though she is no longer on this earth.

What are your hobbies and what do you do to relax?

My hobbies are mostly sporting activities, travels and dancing.

Do you have any favourite quote or saying?

Do what you are good at; do it well with the best you can.

What advice or message do you have for young Africans who want to become entrepreneurs?

Never underestimate your talents; develop them and exploit them.

If you are bored with life, if you don't get up every morning with a burning desire to do things, you don't have enough goals.

- Lou Holtz, Football Coach

ISAIAH OLATUNDE OLADEJI
Solmax Technologies

Dr Isaiah Olatunde Oladeji, a highly innovative scientist and engineer earned his B.Sc and M.Sc in Physics at the University of Ilorin in Nigeria.

He taught at the same university as an Assistant Lecturer in Physics until he was awarded the United States government Fulbright Scholarship to complete his PhD in Physics (condensed matter physics and microelectronics) at the University of Central Florida, Orlando, Florida, USA.

His previous work experience as Scientist/Engineer was with Bell Laboratory of Lucent Technology, USA; Chartered Semiconductor, Singapore (now Global Foundries); ATMEL Corporation, United Kingdom, where he pioneered, setup and commissioned the copper technology manufacturing line. He also invented several semiconductor fabrications processes to facilitate the copper interconnect integration.

He left UK for USA in 2007 to launch his own company, Solmax Technologies LLC, and Sisom Thin Films, LLC. Solmax Technology is an alternative energy company, and Sisom is an advanced materials research and development company. In between, he became Chief Science Officer of Planar Energy, a lithium ion manufacturing company, and one of licensees of the technology he developed in lithium ion battery. Under Sisom, he invented wet electrodeless systems, processes, and precursor formulations for fast direct deposition of nanoparticle-based film on various substrates for the fabrication of solar cells, lithium batteries, sensors, solid oxide fuels cells, and dry biomass.

Dr. Oladeji holds more than 15 issued US patents; he is a 1997 winner of NASA Tech Brief award of technical innovation, and a 2010 nominee of Lemelson-MIT Award.

The Interview:

How did the idea for your business come about?

I stumbled on a solar energy book during my undergraduate days in Nigeria that got me thinking, due especially to the fact that we have abundant sun all year round and yet we lack electricity. Though we were never taught anything solar energy, my independent research lead me to discover that there is a device called solar cell that could convert solar radiation into electricity. All my studies and desire from that moment onwards were devoted to learning how to make solar cells and other energy related devices and have a factory to make them. Thus my PhD dissertation was on solar cells. Solar cells fabrication like other semiconductor devices require high technology, hence a need for substantial starting funds to setup the manufacturing plant. As a fresh poor graduate I had no choice but to join silicon industries. It was only after about 9 years in the silicon industries that I decided to start my own company. This is after having sufficient savings, and tweaking my idea over the years to the point I was convinced it was sellable.

Give the readers some insight into your business?

My company researches and develops advanced materials suitable for the fabrications of various devices that include solar cells, lithium ion batteries, sensors etc. We do contract research for big companies and research labs around the world. When successful we license the developed intellectual properties to those companies and institutions. If the demand of the final product is going to be limited we make it on demand for the company or the lab that paid for the original development.

In your opinion, what do you consider as some of the top skills needed to be a successful entrepreneur?

In my opinion, and for my kind of business, to be successful one needs to be innovative, resourceful, flexible and be able to persevere.

What demographic group would you consider as your key clients?

We deal with companies and labs globally, especially those with line business in advanced materials used in making batteries, solar cells and sensors.

What have been some of your challenges and lessons learned from them?

As a Black owned high tech company, it has been a struggle to raise money from investors, or get business from possible clients. For example we have never been able to raise any money directly through Sisom Thin Films, LLC. All the money we raised to get the company off the ground has been through a third party company. When we eventually did, we have to continuously prove ourselves to existing clients and overcome much higher barrier placed on our path by the new clients.

In today's challenging world, what do you do to stay on top of the game?

Innovate all the time.

What does success mean to you and the best way to achieve long-term success?

Success to me, whether short-term and long-term, is doing what I want to do and getting paid doing it.

What has been your most satisfying moment in business?

When I successfully raised several million dollars in investment and government grant.

How has being an entrepreneur affected your (family) life?

I have had to spend little time with my family on weekends and holidays.

What other sacrifices have you made to be a successful entrepreneur?

Not getting a pay check for a number of years.

On average, how many hours do you work per day and what is your typical day like?

At least 12 hours a day.

Where do you see yourself and business in another 10 years?

I am growing Sisom Thin Films to be acquired by a bigger company within the next 2 to 3 years. I will then be free to go and fully develop my company in Nigeria into energy devices manufacturing and services powerhouse.

What are your guiding personal and business principles?

My personal and business principles are centered on integrity and nothing else.

What is your greatest fear, and how do you manage fear?

In the real sense of it I do not fear anything. This is because I always have plans A, B, C, D, E, F. If Plan A does not work I go to plan B.

What is your best aspect of being an entrepreneur?

The best aspect of being an entrepreneur is that you are your own boss.

Do you have role models and why?

My role model is more in the academic field rather than business. That role model is Maxwell; on how he used some elegant yet simple equations to explain electromagnetic waves. Those fundamental explanations are at the core of the advancement we have today in telecommunications. My ambition is to have such a legacy.

What are your hobbies and what do you do to relax?

I will say none. I relax only by exercising and sleeping.

Do you have any favourite quote or saying?

None.

What advice or message do you have for young Africans who want to become entrepreneurs?

Outside Africa, especially in technology, I will say there is a very rough road out there where your self-confidence will be tested to the limit. If you are not that good and can't handle the snobbery do not try it.

The mediocre teacher tells. The good teacher explains. The superior teacher demonstrates. The great teacher inspires.

- William Arthur Ward, Writer

JACQUELINE CHAVONNE GOLIATH
De Fynne Nursery

Jacqueline Chavonne Goliath is the Managing Director of De Fynne Nursery, an award-winning wholesale grower of Fynbos and Agricultural crops. It has firmly established itself as one of South Africa's Fynbos and Agricultural seedling growing experts.

Jacky (as she's fondly called) grew up in the dusty roads of the rural mission station of Abbotsdale on the West Coast of South Africa, near Cape Town. She got to know of plants at a young age whilst doing gardening of vegetables with her Dad.

She later earned a degree in Horticulture and had various years of experience of work in Africa doing development work in rural communities. Her focus was on the establishment of nurseries in the local communities in countries such as Senegal, Ghana, and Zambia.

Her initial experience in working with South Africa's indigenous crops, have guided and prepared her for the journey that she currently follows.

The Interview:

How did the idea for your business come about?

While working at a NGO, myself and my current business partner, Elton Jefthas, decided to start a nursery of indigenous plants in his back yard to compliment our income. As both of us had experience in working with and growing Fynbos and indigenous plants, the new venture was like a hobby to us. We started with about 1 000 plants. As these plants become sale-able, we were sold out and needed to start from scratch again. We saw that there was a demand for the product and continued growing more plants. As the local communities and businesses became more aware of water-wise gardening, the increase into indigenous and Fynbos plants skyrocketed. As demand increased for our products, we needed to move out of the back yard and moved to bigger premises to supply our needs.

Give the readers some insight into your business?

De Fynne Nursery is a wholesale nursery that grows containerized plants for both the Horticultural and Agricultural sector. This includes indigenous and Fynbos plants, fruit bearing crops such as Blueberries, Strawberries, Granadilla, Citrus, Olive trees, Tomatoes and strawberry plants. We also look after and grow research material such as apples, pears, kiwi, figs and cherries to name a few. De Fynne is a large supplier of products to landscapers, wine estates, retailers and other chain stores which include Woolworths. Since 2001 while starting in a back yard, we are now situated on a 22 hectare farm where we currently have the wholesale nursery, as well as the production of plums for the export market. We employ about 32 people and additional 10 workers in season of the plum season.

In your opinion, what do you consider as some of the top skills needed to be a successful entrepreneur?

A successful entrepreneur must have the skill to plan short and long term. It is important to be able to communicate effectively within the company (staff) and externally (to your clients). It is of outmost important to react to changes in the business, ex market demands, climate change, etc. To successfully manage cash flow is also very important. Be able to lead by example for your staff and other industry players.

What demographic group would you consider as your key clients?

Our key clients includes both the Horticultural and Agricultural sector, which includes both commercial farmers, retail and whole sale nurseries, wine estates and research institutions.

What have been some of your challenges and lessons learned from them?

That you need to react to market demands. That quality is more important than quantities. Word of mouth is your best marketing tool and that communication is key.

In today's challenging world, what do you do to stay on top of the game?

We change with the changes, meaning that we react to market demand, climate change and whatever the need might be. If this season the need is yellow flowers, we grow yellow. Be pro-active rather than reactive. We believe in our product needs to speak for us when we cannot - meaning that we need to supply good quality products and services at all times. At all times try to come up with new products that give you that edge against your competitors. Also try to add value as far as possible.

What does success mean to you and the best way to achieve long-term success?

Success is to see that not only your business, but your staff grows with you. If your staff members are happy and comfortable in their work environment, your business will also flourish. Success is also to be financially sustainable and to grow your profit and market demand on a yearly basis. The best way to achieve long term success will be to believe in what you do and strive for perfection.

What has been your most satisfying moment in business?

There has been a few. One of my most satisfying moments in business was to secure a growing contract with a large chain store to supply plants to them on an annual basis. With a very high standard and quality criteria, we as a small business feel proud to be associated with this chain store for more than 6 years now. Another one was moving to bigger premises, thus growing from 1,5 to 22 hectares within a year. This gave us the opportunity to expand our business and create more employment. Another satisfying moment was to be awarded the 2015 Toyota New Harvest of the Year award. Being compared and competing against other large commercial farmers, made me feel very good and proud of being a farmer.

How has being an entrepreneur affected your (family) life?

I am not married and stay on the farm where the business is. It is very difficult for me to have normal working hours, as even on weekends there is always something to attend to for example a broken irrigation pipe. As working with plants is my passion, I enjoy doing what I do. The rest of my family has learned to adapt to my lifestyle and is also experiencing and starting to live more closely to nature, since I stay on the farm, thus being more aware of the effects nature have on the plants. Due to my long working hours, I do spend very little time with my family.

What other sacrifices have you made to be a successful entrepreneur?

My business has become a lifestyle to me. As I stay on the farm I find it difficult to "switch off". Thus always on the look-out for anything that could go wrong on the farm, even after hours and weekends. I therefore do sacrifice a lot of my personal time. Starting small, a lot of financial sacrifices were also done to grow the business. To be successful, you need to be able to make sacrifices.

On average, how many hours do you work per day and what is your typical day like?

About 12 hours per day in winter, and about 14 hours per day in the summer. In the morning I would meet up with my production manager and discuss the day's work. I would then visit the different production areas on the farm to make sure that all is up to standard. This can take up to 2 hours of my time, after which I would then go to my office to adhere to administration work and e-mails or meetings that have been set up. At 17h00 when my staff leaves the farm, I will feed the dogs and take some time to relax. After about 3 hours I will go back to my office to continue working and finish off my day.

Where do you see yourself and business in another 10 years?

I do hope that I would have an early retirement☺. But I doubt if that will ever happen. I do see that De Fynne will be more sustainable and have a bigger market share. I do see that we will be creating more job opportunities for the surrounding communities. During that time, we will be making use of higher technologies and be able to add more value to our current products.

What are your guiding personal and business principles?

If you want the world /community to be a better place, you need to lead by example. Treat other people as you would like to be treated. We as De Fynne believe in empowering our employees and building their capacity. It keeps them motivated and builds their personal capacity as well.

Our company's mission is to provide a consistent supply of high quality indigenous and agricultural plants to the nursery, retail and landscaping industry in South Africa. To provide nursery growing experience/skills and infrastructure as a Contract Grower of niche market plants.

What is your greatest fear, and how do you manage fear?

I am blessed to have a business partner that motivates me in time of trials. To stay focused I constantly surround myself with positive people and spaces. Also to live close to my Creator and believing in a higher power helps me to stay motivated and strong in my doings.

What is your best aspect of being an entrepreneur?

The passion and commitment that I have towards the business, makes it easier to sacrifice long and unbearable working hours.

Do you have role models and why?

Yes. My parents are my biggest role models. I grew up in a very conservative household that believes in Ubuntu - "I am because we are" and were formed with the inputs and guidance of my family. We were taught and had been raised in a very humble household, but were very proud of our belongings, though very minimal. This has taught me to go through life to strive for the best, but to survive with what I have. My parents have also taught us to believe in ourselves, no matter how hard the struggle.

What are your hobbies and what do you do to relax?

I have 2 German shepherd dogs which mean the world to me. I relax by taking long walks with them on the farm, as well as taking pictures of nature and the surroundings. I also often go to the West Coast beach just to enjoy the environment.

Do you have any favourite quote or saying?

"Be the change you wish to see in the world" - Mahatma Gandhi

What advice or message do you have for young Africans who want to become entrepreneurs?

You must have a passion for what you are doing. It is your passion for what you do that will carry you through your problems or struggles. Your passion could be turned into a profit gaining business. Believe in yourselves, your product and what you do. Go for quality rather than for quantity. Being an entrepreneur is not easy, but is very fulfilling. It is unfortunately not an 8 a.m. to 5 p.m., or a weekend job, but a lifestyle... enjoy it!

You cannot swim for new horizons until you have courage to lose sight of the shore.

- William Faulkner, writer

JASON NJOKU
iROKO

Jason Njoku is the Chief Executive Officer and a Co-founder of iROKO, one of the early video-on-demand movie platforms for Nigerian movies, otherwise known as Nollywood.

Nollywood studios produce thousands of movies every year and its viewers cut across all nationalities in sub-Sahara Africa. Fortune's estimate of Nollywood in 2014 was a $3 billion industry, ahead of Hollywood in terms of volume.

iROKO remains one of the country's largest internet and entertainment companies in Africa, reaching out to millions of movie lovers around the globe and around the clock with hit movies and original TV series. It does this seamlessly through its own iROKO apps, TV channels and a network of global distribution partnership.

The Interview:

How did the idea for your business come about?
I was back home living with mum, and she asked me to go and fetch her some more Nollywood movies. As a child of the internet, I started my search online and found nothing - nowhere to either buy or stream the films, which I thought was odd. That was the genesis of iROKO. I started researching the industry, found a gap in the market, and the rest is history.

Give the readers some insight into your business?

iROKO is the home of Nollywood - through our platforms and channels, we show and distribute the best Nigerian movies and TV series to fans all over the world. We have offices in Lagos, London and New York, and a team of over 100, making sure we deliver awesome content.

In your opinion, what do you consider as some of the top skills needed to be a successful entrepreneur?

Ingenuity, you need to be a self starter, you need to think differently from everyone else. You need the ability to cut out the noise and the distractions and focus on your company.

What demographic group would you consider as your key clients?

Our customers come from all walks of life - anyone who loves being entertained and who loves Nollywood is a potential customer.

What have been some of your challenges and lessons learned from them?

Starting an internet business in Nigeria comes with a very unique set of challenges. In the early days, it was the simple things like internet connections. We couldn't get enough bandwidth to upload the movies so I had to jump on a plane back to the UK with a bunch of films and upload them there. When we started to grow the team, finding the right talent to deliver what we wanted to achieve as a company was also difficult, as many of the roles we were recruiting for were relatively new for the country; sourcing the right talent was a massive challenge. This was not insurmountable though, and over the years we've built an awesome team both in Lagos and in New York.

In today's challenging world, what do you do to stay on top of the game?

I make sure I think ahead - so I try not to just simply fire-fight daily problems. I look into where our audience / where the market is going to be in 6 months' time and then make sure the company is ready for that eventuality.

What does success mean to you and the best way to achieve long-term success?

The company is still going and reaching new heights after five years, in an emerging market that hasn't really truly come online yet, so in that respect, I see this as a relative success. Is there more success planned for the future? Absolutely - we're still a young company with plenty of ambition to become the dominant pan-Africa entertainment brand. How can we achieve this? By continuing to work harder and faster than everyone else, by continuing to develop partnerships with other leading global brands and by making sure we continue to out our customers first. we never, ever stray too far away from our customers, we're obsessed with taking on and implementing their input. After all, they're the ones who have brought us this far.

What has been your most satisfying moment in business?

Difficult to say; I'm fortunate enough to have recorded a few great wins, but I must say, closing on our first round, Series A investment from Tiger Global back in 2010 was a mic-drop moment. It was at that point I really thought, yes - this Nollywood thing has legs. Let's see what we can do with it now.

How has being an entrepreneur affected your (family) life?

It's most definitely a struggle to balance everything. Such is the nature of my work. I often spend more time on a plane than I do with my kids, and that's not easy. But the time I do spend with my wife and children is amazing - we're very tight, they are very understanding and we have amazing quality time together.

What other sacrifices have you made to be a successful entrepreneur?

Everything - health, relationships with friends and loved ones, sleep… In the early days, I had nothing - no money, no girlfriend, no new clothes etc. It was work and work only. Very few people are actually willing to give up life's fripperies - I was happy to do so as I had an end goal in mind, but I can't lie, it wasn't easy at all.

On average, how many hours do you work per day and what is your typical day like?

It can be anything up to 18 hours a day. It also depends on where I am in the world; what my travel schedule is looking like. Essentially, I very rarely just switch off, especially as we have teams across different time zones. Contrary to popular belief, a 'typical day' isn't in any way glamorous. I'm glued to my laptop. I very rarely leave the office. I don't do mingle with the stars or do any red carpet events. I try and get out in Lagos and meet other entrepreneurs / start-ups when I can.

Where do you see yourself and business in another 10 years?

We shall see! iROKO will be in a very different place then.

What are your guiding personal and business principles?

Hard work!

What is your best aspect of being an entrepreneur?

Building a company that I'm proud of is an amazing feeling.

Do you have role models and why?

I read a lot of other entrepreneurs' biographies. I admire their hustle, their creativity and also learn from their mistake; how they overcame challenges and also, how they brokered their biggest and best deals.

What are your hobbies and what do you do to relax?

I have always loved going to the cinema so that's the main thing I do to relax.

What advice or message do you have for young Africans who want to become entrepreneurs?

Prepare for battle, if you decide to set up your own business. Don't get distracted by the small things in life and don't think you'll cosy down to a 9-5-type lifestyle. Prepare for the fact that your business will be your best friend, family, lover, enemy and everything else.

Your internal beliefs are what drive your success.

- Ron Willingham

JOSELYNE UMUTONIWASE
Rwanda Clothing

Joselyne Umutoniwase is a fashion Designer, film director and editor and has worked in the Rwandan film industry for five years prior to starting Rwanda Clothing. She is also the creative mind behind the brand.

The company is designed to become a fashion revolution by establishing a Rwandan style and fashion identity. It designs and produces a high-quality collection that is expected to change the perception of fashion and the buying behaviour of people in Rwanda and in the whole Africa.

"Rwanda Clothing is the Rwandan fashion brand and will be one of the world market leaders of African fashion in terms of design and quality of our products as well as our brand popularity and recognition. "It will become the first known fashion producer from Africa worldwide and a pioneer in creating a brand new market segment: African fashion international."

The Interview:

How did the idea for your business come about?

The idea started in 2010 when I was invited as one of Rwandan female filmmakers by the German government and the German film director Volker Schlöndorff to participate in a scholarship programme in Berlin and Mainz. I was determined to take with me a piece of Africa. Since, I have been creating outfits for myself; I wanted to see if people would appreciate my creativity. By luck, people there were very interested in my designs and even started purchasing the pieces I took with me so that was the beginning of my career. As it turned out, people in my home country like my designs as well.

Give the readers some insight into your business?

Rwanda Clothing started as a small outfit and that's how I wanted it. I wanted something that I would be able to manage and grow organically. From only two tailors, the company has gradually grown to the point where we now have about 20 employees in four years.

In your opinion, what do you consider as some of the top skills needed to be a successful entrepreneur?

In my own case, determination, patience and talent plays a big role in the success of the company. Generally, people should try to see beyond obstacles and get a clearer picture of how they want to grow.

What have been some of your challenges and lessons learned from them?

At the beginning, it was impatience. With all my talent, beautiful outfits and creations, the market was still small and I had to learn how to determine who my clients were. What I could offer them to make the right connection with them and to have them become loyal customers.

The second was skills as it was very difficult to find the right people who could work with me; one reason I decided to start small and grow the team slowly.

The last point was sticking to the plan. I wanted to offer high-end custom-made clothes but with lack of customers who knew what that meant, I started thinking of changing the plan. Luckily, things worked well before I could change the plan and I never had to change what I really believed in.

In today's challenging world, what do you do to stay on top of the game?

It requires two things: improvement and innovation of the product. Make sure that the customs you started with stays with you and not only to keep offering the best, but also to keep your rules.

What does success mean to you and the best way to achieve long-term success?

For me, it's the fulfilment of a dream. To be able to succeed despite the odds and obstacles. It means to be the best in something and become an inspiration for others.

What has been your most satisfying moment in business?

This was when I realised that, yes it is possible; yes I can make it and also when I see people come to me and say that I inspire them and give them courage to do something.

How has being an entrepreneur affected your (family) life?

Being an entrepreneur has been a challenge in terms of juggling between family life and the everyday work. However, I knew I wanted both and I knew I had to double work to be able to make both work. It is still a challenge, but that's what makes it more exciting for me.

What other sacrifices have you made to be a successful entrepreneur?

As an entrepreneur, the sacrifices are endless and you

need to keep facing them every day. I got married a year before I started the company; then I decided not to have kids until the company got to a point where I could get a break. I didn't know when but I decided that in order to make it a success, I had to do it that way. After 4 years, it became a reality, and now I have a beautiful baby girl and the company is still going stronger and stronger.

On average, how many hours do you work per day and what is your typical day like?

A designer actually works 24/7 because your brain is always on duty and you are always trying to figure out how this or that can work. You finish your first collection and immediately start thinking of the next one; so it is hard to tell how many hours. I work 6 days a week.

Where do you see yourself and business in another 10 years?

I see myself as a mentor and a well known entrepreneur in Africa and around the world. The company will also become well established and well known in Africa.

What are your guiding personal and business principles?

To stay true to yourself, and don't be afraid to stand out and follow your heart. For the company, we stick to our rules and make sure people understand our goals.

What is your greatest fear, and how do you manage fear?

My greatest fear was not be able to manage the company as it grows bigger and bigger. However, I found out that as the company grow, I have to grow with it and learn a lot to be able to manage it.

What is your best aspect of being an entrepreneur?

I don't give up easily and I keep learning every single day.

Do you have role models and why?

They are many and they are people who inspire me to become a strong woman and a successful entrepreneur. Like strong women in fashion business who make things look possible and achievable.
People like Donna Karan, Diane von Furstenberg, Coco Chanel, Stella McCartney, Vera Wang, and many others.

What are your hobbies and what do you do to relax?

To relax, I love reading and listening to music. I also love writing and may be one day, I will write a novel.

Do you have any favourite quote or saying?

"If you believe in yourself you have all the power it takes to achieve it" - my own quote.

What advice or message do you have for young Africans who want to become entrepreneurs?

If you believe in yourself you have all the power it take to achieve it; so go for it. Try, try, try and don't ever give up!

Never look down to test the ground before taking your next step; only he who keeps his eye fixed on the far horizon will find his right road.

- Dag Hammerskjőld

JOSEPH VAN APPIA
Van Appia & Van Der Lee law firm

Joseph van Appia is a top Dutch lawyer who specialises in immigration and criminal law. In fact, he's the first African lawyer in The Netherlands and one of the founders of Van Appia & Van Der Lee law firm in the city of Amsterdam.

Born in Ghana, he moved to The Netherlands at the age of 18; where he had his university education in law. Soon after, he established his own law office.

The Interview:

What informed your decision to become a lawyer?

I guess I'm following my family tradition, as law profession runs in my blood. My great-grandfather was a lawyer, so was my grandfather; my uncle was also a lawyer. Even here in The Netherlands, my sister's daughter is also a lawyer. I remember when I was a kid, my father once told me I would likely become a lawyer because I loved to argue. Ofcourse it was his assumption then, but when I completed my university education, I thought to myself that Africans here have specific problems and an African lawyer would likely be in a better position to deal with their legal problems. It would also be a good way to help my fellow Africans.

How long has Van Appia & Van der Lee law firm been around and what are your areas of specialisation?

My legal firm has been around for a very long time and it's in fact one of the oldest law firms where all the partners have continued to work together. It's quite common in this business for working partners to go their different ways after sometime. We have been together since 1989 but moved to current office in 2001. We actually studied together at the university and the idea of coming together as partners was muted at the university.

With all the partners coming from different backgrounds, how did you manage to make your partnership work so well?

Coming to the country at a young age; to learn the language and become a practising lawyer makes my situation a unique one. I was the first person from Black Africa to become a lawyer and a practising one in The Netherlands. I have worked to earn the respect of my partners, colleagues in law as well as the Judges in front of whom I argue cases. It's quite easy to work and blend well with everyone.

How do you define your uniqueness?

Unique in the sense that where I come from, Ghana, is not a former colony of The Netherlands; meaning that I had to start from the scratch, starting with the ABC of the language and to finally set up a law firm that employs several lawyers instead of me working for another law firm. It would probably have been much easier if I came from say, the Suriname or Antillean that has similar language and background as The Netherlands.

Where is your law firm today compared to when you started?

Well, we have grown, having started with only two lawyers. I personally have two areas of specialisation which are immigration and criminal cases. My colleague next door does family law; two other ladies here work on immigration related cases. There's also another lady that handles criminal and taxation cases.

What makes your law firm different from others?

We are quite different in the sense that its one of the law firms with partners that have been together for a long time without breaking up. We have a very good name and the know-how. Our clients come from all walks of life, Africans, Asians and all. For instance, I once got a call from Amsterdam Schiphol airport from an Indian man who got caught for using a false passport. During my meeting with him, I asked him how he got my contact and he told me that when he got caught, he called his sister in India who in turn gave him my telephone number. This is the type of good reputation that follows our law firm.

What is your typical day like as a lawyer?

It's quite busy and sometimes stressful but that goes with the work. Imagine getting a court case at 2 p.m. and another one at 3 p.m. with possibly only 15 minutes between cases. I also have to drive around a lot to meet clients in faraway places and sometimes have to juggle these between court cases.

What are the challenges of the legal profession in The Netherlands?

Professionally, it's not a huge challenge, because I prepare for my cases. However, I often have to chase some clients around to pay for legal work rendered to them. This was especially at the beginning when most clients ran off without paying, but with time, you learn not to give too much leeway and that's not a problem anymore.

As a minority lawyer arguing a case for a minority clients, do you use racial profiling for instance to support your case?

I don't use my background or that of my clients. I only argue my cases on the basis of argument and law. At the end of the day, it's about the argument you put forward that will help you win a case. I think I have the ability and the knowledge to argue my cases in convincing manner.

Do you see yourself as a role model for Africans in Europe and if so, why?

Yes, I do. I often go to elementary and secondary schools and to some universities to give lectures, using myself as an example, to let the students know that they can achieve whatever goals they set out for themselves. For instance, some Africans often say that they don't have any chance of success here, but the fact is there are challenges and obstacles everywhere and I often look at the positive side and less on the negative. Even in Africa, we discriminate among ourselves, so what's the point in using that as an excuse here. If you make yourself productive in any society, you get respect, but if you end up stealing or committing crimes, it's your fault. True, there may be some discrimination here and there, but overlook it and move on. In my opinion, life is what you make of it.

What do you do to relax?

I do a lot of sports. I cycle long distance few times a week. For instance I regularly circle up to 40 km and every summer, I often cycle 90 km to and back from my mother's place once a week. Other times, I go to the gym. That's how I relax!

What is your advice and message to Africans in The Netherlands and Europe in general?

Try to gather yourself up, don't think because you are a minority here, success is not possible because that's not true. Try to put whatever setbacks that you may have behind you. Most importantly, try to invest in yourself! Investing in yourself means sacrificing few years of your life here to go to school, instead of the urge to make money quickly by doing menial jobs only, which in the long term only earns you little. Investing in meaningful studies gives you the capacity and ability to do better in life.

In reading the lives of great men, I found that the first victory they won was over themselves... Self-discipline with all of them came first.

- Harry S. Truman, 33rd U.S. President

KAMAL BUDHABHATTI
Craft Silicon

Kamal Budhabhatti is the founder and Chief Executive Officer of Craft Silicon, a Kenya-based global software development and services company.

Craft Silicon has been recognised as one of the Africa's biggest software house across the emerging markets with offices in India, Nigeria and the USA. Craft Silicon has talent strength comprising 300+ technology architects, and domain experts, providing solutions to the banking, financial services and insurance industries, and Mobile Commerce.

It's able to provide varied technological solutions across many continents in different languages like English, French, Arabic and Spanish.

The Interview:

How did the idea for your business come about?

After I completed my studies in India, I moved to Kenya and

worked for a company in the polythene sector for a while doing data entry. Five months later, a friend approached me to write software for a local bank. Of course my boss found out about this and was not very pleased. As a result, he had me deported back to India. On the flight, all I could think about was the great opportunities in Kenya. In no time, I moved back to Kenya and began writing software for banks full time. This eventually gave birth to what Craft Silicon is today.

Give the readers some insight into your business?

Craft Silicon is a 360-degree BFSI technology companies with end-to-end solution for core banking software processors for commercial and micro finance banks, mobile commerce platforms as well as e-commerce. At Craft Silicon, we believe that the next-generation architecture for banking should be such that it manages the dynamic nature of the business and technology, while supporting agility, fostering innovation and being flexible. We have robust solutions with a quality implementation and support expertise that helps financial institution to enhance their operations. We serve a customer base of more than 250 institutions across 45 countries.

In your opinion, what do you consider as some of the top skills needed to be a successful entrepreneur?

Passion and love for what you do!

What demographic group would you consider as your key clients?

Our vision is very simple: to be a world leader in whatever we do. At Craft Silicon, we like to embrace creativity while focusing on long-term goals. Business that lacks a creative edge is bound to tumble along the way. Passion, integrity and innovation are our key strength to achieve our vision.

What have been some of your challenges and lessons learned from them?

Craft Silicon faced hard times at its initial stages of the operation. It was difficult to establish credibility as only few people trusted us. Most of the time, people didn't know what they wanted until we showed it to them.

In today's challenging world, what do you do to stay on top of the game?

Innovation is the backbone of this business. If we are not innovative, we will be out of business. For a company that has established itself in an emerging market, it is very difficult to compete with the big boys in developed economies. The only advantage is that we have a unique set of challenges in emerging markets and we must find ways of solving them. Solutions to problems in emerging economies should emanate from the emerging markets as there is a better understanding of the challenges.

What does success mean to you and the best way to achieve long-term success?

Like everybody success excites me, but I like to focus on long-term goals. This is because when you write software it takes a fairly long time before it starts to generate returns. I also think passion, integrity, having a transparent culture and innovation have played a critical role. I have always ensured that my team love their work.

What has been your most satisfying moment in business?

I believe highly in empowering humanity. This way, we have established the Craft Silicon Foundation to empower people in slum areas. We have a bus that goes to Kibera, Mathare, Huruma and Kangemi among others. It is fully equipped with computers powered by solar panels and offers free computer classes to the public. We also run free computer classes at our headquarters where over 6000 students have benefited. Many of them have gone ahead to become professionals, besides developing their own businesses such as cyber cafes.

How has being an entrepreneur affected your (family) life?

Home time is insanely low. My spouse and my daughter will forgive me. But I try my level best to give them some quality time every day.

What other sacrifices have you made to be a successful entrepreneur?

When you love what do you like me, there is nothing I feel that I am sacrificing. Love demands and I give what it demands on all grounds.

On average, how many hours do you work per day and what is your typical day like?

My day starts according to its requirement by higher chance. But on a typical day, I start at 8 in the morning with guided decisions and discussions on product development and help think through how to build out the business and sales. Then I get settled in the mobile innovation square, where I spend another 8-10 hours working with the team to design and build a next-generation payments and B2C platforms and solutions.

Where do you see yourself and business in another 10 years?

For sure, Craft Silicon will be a US$500 million company. I see it as a next-generation services company that offers all kinds of amazing and innovative software solutions to the world. I want Craft Silicon to be a leading and respectable IT organisation.

What are your guiding personal and business principles?

My parents have been very supportive. The customers who believed in me when I started out were influential in our growth and success. Thanks to them, we are where we are today. My staff has also helped me to deliver what is expected of us. I also admire Steve Jobs for his focus, his tenacity, and passion.

What is your greatest fear, and how do you manage fear?

The market is very competitive and therefore we have to be innovative to remain relevant. This is what I think about a lot, how to stay ahead and innovation is the key to this.

What is your best aspect of being an entrepreneur?

I have a lot of personal, heartfelt relationships. Many customers who are CEOs are my friends for a very long time. There is a personal element to all my relationships. Life is too short not to be real at relationships.

Do you have role models and why?

Bill Gates, for obvious reasons!

What are your hobbies and what do you do to relax?

I enjoy long drives; the scenery is just magnificent. I also like to play with my daughter.

Do you have any favourite quote or saying?

In the good old times and in the words of Robert frost: "…I have promises to keep, and miles to go before I sleep; and miles to go before I sleep."

And in the new age: "Sometimes when you innovate, you make mistakes. It is best to admit them quickly, and get on with improving your other innovations." - Steve Jobs"

What advice or message do you have for young Africans who want to become entrepreneurs?

They should stay focused and deliver value for money and success will come as a by-product. They should not look at short-term goals - ditch the 'get rich quick' mentality. To be successful, a long-term strategy is inevitable.

Success seems to be largely a matter of hanging on after others have let go.

- William Feather, publisher

KASOPE LADIPO-AJAI
OmoAlata Food Services

Kasope Ladipo-Ajai is the founder and Chief Executive Officer of OmoAlata, a Nigerian food service brand focused on the production and sale of hygienically processed and packaged local soups, spices and peppers.

The company sell wholesale to supermarkets, including packages of pre-ordered volumes, specified blending levels and specific mix for delivery to any location in the country for homes, hotels and other events.

The name OmoAlata literally means 'Son or Daughter of a Spice Seller', which symbolizes a native name given to local street wise kids from the Yoruba tribe in Nigeria. It is also used to depict someone funky but in a local or native way.

Kasope Ladipo-Ajai who has a BSc in Computer Science and a PGd in Strategic Business IT said: "I am a young and independent Nigerian woman who has adopted a far reaching outlook to life. "I respect and appreciate my roots but refuse to be boxed in by dogmatic customs or expectations. "I always try to find a 'smarter' way to solve problems and never believed in laborious, conformist methods. "I have gathered years of people/project management experience from different areas of business; from working 4 years with Virgin Nigeria as Project coordinator & Business/Process Analyst to being an IT Service Engineer with Taytom Group."

The Interview:

How did the idea for your business come about?

Seeing Nigerian food ingredients in ethnic stores in the UK & USA with "Made in Ghana" labels ignited a longing to change the narrative that, "Nothing good comes out of Naija."

Give the readers some insight into your business?

OmoAlata (McPeppers) is a Nigerian food service brand focused on the production and sale of hygienically processed and packaged local Nigerian soups, spices and peppers. OmoAlata peppermix is a smooth blend of farm fresh peppers, onions & tomatoes which has been parboiled and frozen in ready-to-use pouches. Nigeria has a growing population of over 170 million people. Based on our local research, it is evident that a large proportion of Nigerians eat soups and stews daily.

The process of making these meals require several

preparatory steps, and on average, this process takes at least 2-3 hours. Presently, only a few products in the Nigerian market offer a ready-to-cook blend for Nigerian soup or stew.

OmoAlata seeks to offer products to Nigerians, home and abroad, who are either too busy to buy, sort and blend pepper or need a convenient way to make their choice Nigerian soups.
There is an existing gap in local food processing and storage in Nigeria, and we aspire to bridge the gap in the value chain for farm fresh peppers. This will in turn reduce post-harvest loss of local farmers and create more job opportunities in the agro-allied industry. Finally, we hope to use our strong local brand identity to position an African product range that will sit in stores all over the world for Nigerians and other customers present in these markets.

In your opinion, what do you consider as some of the top skills needed to be a successful entrepreneur?

Perseverance; Risk Taking,; Versatility

What demographic group would you consider as your key clients?

OmoAlata Pepper Mix is mainly for urban students, workers or entrepreneurs between the ages of 18 & 45 who would appreciate convenience and are able to pay for it. It is also for event planners or cooks looking to purchase tomato products at a discounted price to cater for the volume necessary for their events.

In today's challenging world, what do you do to stay on top of the game?

I am constantly reading and looking for information on how to improve my business. Motion is the only way to stay alive and relevant.

What does success mean to you and the best way to achieve long-term success?

Success is achieving those "impossible" and "unrealistic"

goals you have set for yourself. It is best to build your success organically. You make mistakes, grow slowly and firmly build roots which cannot be displaced at the slightest wind.

What has been your most satisfying moment in business?

Winning 'She Leads Africa' award. It was humbling and positively reinforcing.

How has being an entrepreneur affected your (family) life?

I have a very supportive family. Everyone helps out when they can and very understanding when for example I miss family functions because of work. They see how much passion and hard work I put into my business and support me all the way.

What other sacrifices have you made to be a successful entrepreneur?

I am an IT person by formal profession. I have had to put my fast rising, lucrative career on hold to chase my dreams. I have had to cut back on my socializing as every penny I get is invested in my business.

On average, how many hours do you work per day and what is your typical day like?

8 to 12 hours on an average. Wake up, check my mails, respond to urgent ones before 7 a.m., sort out family meals etc. Go to my factory or meetings or my office and face piled up paperwork (invoices, staff reports etc). Follow-up/meet with sales team, make and receive numerous phone calls, get home around 8 -9 pm. Sort out meals, run through to-do list, try to finish things not yet done, go to bed around 12 midnight to 1 a.m.

Where do you see yourself and business in another 10 years?

We plan to retail in all the big food chains in Nigeria such as Shoprite, Spar, Justrite, Goodies, CityDia etc. We would sit in foreign chain stores in the US, UK and rest of Europe such as Walmart, Aldi, Asda, Kroger, Dia etc. We would be a Public Limited Liability company.

What are your guiding personal and business principles?

Nothing good comes easy. Inanimate objects can never outsmart me. Do your absolute best and the rest will fall in place. Know when to take a break.

What is your best aspect of being an entrepreneur?

The opportunity to be creative and think outside the box. I am not restricted by any formal institutions' or workplace bureaucracies or politics.

What are your hobbies and what do you do to relax?

I love to design spaces, I love cooking and I love travelling.

Do you have any favourite quote or saying?

Life is too short to be a mediocre.

What advice or message do you have for young Africans who want to become entrepreneurs?

There is never a right time to quit your job and pursue your dreams. Take the plunge; never be afraid of failing, its part of being successful. Just push on and try again!

Never be bullied into silence; never allow yourself to be made a victim. Accept no one's definition of your life; define yourself.

- Harvey Fierstein

KELVIN MACHARIA KURIA
Sunrise Tracking

26-year-old Kelvin Macharia Kuria is the founder and Chief Executive Officer of Sunrise Tracking, a company that offers security solutions for both vehicles and buildings.

Kelvin is an undergraduate student pursuing Bachelors of Commerce at the University of Nairobi. He is also a Global Scholar under (GSP-2011) in Entrepreneurship and Leadership from Africa Leadership Academy in South Africa.

Kelvin has earned numerous accolades, including the Kenyan Youth Ambassador for The Road to Nairobi 2016 project, a project that seeks to promote the Sustainable Development Goals (SDGs) No.8; named for the second consecutive year 2015 and 2016 in the Forbes list of Africa's Top 30 Under 30 most promising Young Entrepreneur in Africa; 100 Most Influential Young Africans under Science and Technology category that focused on young Africans who are leading the innovation revolution across the continent; top 40 under 40 men in Kenya through Business Daily; East Africa regional winner of the CEO Global Titans-Building the nations award and top CIO100 East Africa Awards 3 times consecutively from 2013 to 2015 among many others.

The Interview:

How did the idea for your business come about?

I had just cleared high school, then I travelled to Kenya's capital city of Nairobi, the largest economy in East Africa. Despite the glitz and glamour of a growing city there was an underlying bitter truth of carjacking growing at an alarming rate. According to the crime statistics, there were 50 vehicles car jacked per day. No sooner had my uncle became casualty of carjacking that I identified an opportunity to create the first mobile based car tracking solution to assist vehicle owners control their cars and to reduce chances of carjacking from their phones from wherever they are. With a capital of $300 that I had saved from my pocket money while at school, I was able to design and produce the first 2 mobile based prototypes that I sold and kept reinvesting the profit till today.

Give the readers some insight into your business?

Sunrise Tracking offer authentic and innovative security solutions for both vehicles and buildings such as car tracking products, fleet/fuel management system, CCTV surveillance and biometrics products, in a manner that meet our clients' requirement. In short, we help individuals and companies track vehicles, valuable assets or personnel through our real-time easy-to-use internet based software. We also ensure that our services are to customers' satisfaction at a budgeted cost with reduced overheads. We serve the Kenyan market, with a highly skilled technical team and latest GPS/GPRS/GSM technology which covers the entire global position.

In your opinion, what do you consider as some of the top skills needed to be a successful entrepreneur?

Focus: After setting a long term vision, knowing how to "laser focus" on the very next step to get closer to the ultimate goal. There are so many distracting forces when trying to build a business that this skill is not easy to master.
Resiliency: The ability to weather the ups and downs of any business since it hardly go exactly as planned.
Sell: Every entrepreneur is a sales person whether they want to be or not. They are either selling their ideas, products or services to customers, investors or employees. They work to be there when customers are ready to buy. Alternatively, they know how to let go and move on when they are not.
Learn: Successful entrepreneurs realise they don't know everything and the market is constantly changing. They stay up to date on new systems, technology, and industry trends.
Self-reflection: Allow downtime to reflect on the past and plan for the future. Always working only leads to burnout physically and emotionally.

What demographic group would you consider as your key clients?

30-55 years old; middle income class living in major cities of Nairobi, Nakuru, Mombasa, Eldorect, Kisumu etc.

What have been some of your challenges and lessons learned from them?

Having graduated from low class to middle class level, they invest in buying vehicles and mortgages or building houses. They then become a soft target for carjacking and house break-ins since they have been observed growing from one level to the next.

In today's challenging world, what do you do to stay on top of the game?

Using innovation to standardize for easy growth of the value chain.

What does success mean to you and the best way to achieve long-term success?

Creating an experience and brand that my clients want to relate with at all time. Using human-centred design thinking process to create a solution that is customizable and to fulfil the promise made to the clients.

How has being an entrepreneur affected your (family) life?

Entrepreneurship is always a lonely journey as a result of the commitment to it. I have ended up losing frequent connections with family members.

What other sacrifices have you made to be a successful entrepreneur?

Losing social life since I'm always working round the clock.

On average, how many hours do you work per day and what is your typical day like?

15 hours. I sleep between 1 a.m. or 2 a.m.; wake up between 5 a.m. and 6 a.m.; arrive office at 8 a.m.; work till 10 p.m. and extend work to home office till 12 a.m.

Where do you see yourself and business in another 10 years?

To become the biggest supplier of innovative security solution with impact to community development and protection of people's assets across Africa.

What are your guiding personal and business principles?

Being organised: Organised minds are clear, and clear

minds take action towards clear objectives. I am always organised and as clear as possible in my life and business affairs. It all start with my desk and work area, then with my plans and actions.

Being Dedicated: I am always dedicated to my personal objectives and business goals which always keep me in line.

Being Dependable: I meet all of my business, social and moral obligations punctually, honestly and honourably. I'm always the "go to" person and the "go to" business; I never have to worry about having to generate extra leads or word-of-mouth referrals.

Being Alert: I open myself to new ideas, experiences and people who can teach me something new - and stay out of ruts and routines. This is one of the best ways I get aware and focused on new opportunities.

Being Optimistic: I leave past failures in the past and focus positively on my future. I am not a glass-half-empty person; I see the glass as being half-full. Life and business are more enjoyable this way.

What is your greatest fear, and how do you manage fear?

Fear of failing; fearing is not a good thing but also it's important to help us make critical decisions. I run away from fear of failing by understanding the situation and analyzing how best to evade it with learning lessons.

What is your best aspect of being an entrepreneur?

1. Making my own decisions. I answer to no one and I thrive on the fact that the success of my business depends on me. Getting to experience the impact of my choices day in and day out fills me with confidence and keeps me on my toes.
2. Meeting and working with remarkable people. I feel like I've gotten to know some of the most interesting people in the world - many of whom are entrepreneurs like myself. It's a fantastic community.
3. Limitless income potential. How much money I make is up to me.

4. Freedom. For me, the ability to live where I want and go on vacation as I please has been invaluable.

Do you have role models and why?

Yes, I do. Tony Elumelu, Akon, Richard Branson, Fred Swankier: Because they challenge and motivate me to bring change and create impact to the society other than just to make money.

What are your hobbies and what do you do to relax?

When I'm free, I'm doing online research, listening to music and watching local contents.

Do you have any favourite quote or saying?

Entrepreneurship is living a few years of your life like most people won't, so that you can spend the rest of your life like most people can't. The future of the African youth lies in a prosperous Africa, not at the bottom of the Mediterranean Sea. Africa hosts the world's youngest population.

What advice or message do you have for young Africans who want to become entrepreneurs?

Everyone has ideas. They may be too busy or lack the confidence or technical ability to carry them out. To carry them out, it is a matter of getting up and doing it. Twenty years from now you will be more disappointed by the things that you didn't do than by the ones you did do. So throw off the bowlines; sail away from the safe harbour; catch the trade winds in your sails; explore; dream and discover!

Rough diamonds may sometimes be mistaken for worthless pebbles.

- Thomas Browne

LILIAN MAKOI
Jamii Africa & WaterTek Africa

Lilian Makoi is the founder of Jamii Africa and co-Founder of WaterTek Africa.

Jamii is a micro-health insurance product for the informal sector. Through innovation and technology, it provides eight different cover options for customers, depending on the number of people in the family. Service options can also be customized for user's unique requirements. Similarly, WaterTek Africa provide water to the underprivileged through the use of technology. It's a digital water supply management platform for governments, NGOs, private organisations and donor funded water projects in Africa. Users utilize digital cards that enables them pay for their water bills prior to usage, allowing for transparency.

Before focusing on entrepreneurship, Makoi who holds a masters degree in International Business, spent about 6 years in the telecom and IT industry.

The Interview:

How did the idea for your business come about?

My house help of four years lost her husband in a motorcycle accident. It was not because the accident was severe, but because at that time, they couldn't afford $25 to access medical help. The hospital staff wouldn't give him any first-aid or treatment until his family paid the hospital deposit. His death cost his children their future. It was a wake-up call for me that something had to be done to the vulnerable and ignored population. Hence the idea of mobile micro-health insurance that is 100% for the low income and informal sector, Jamii Africa.
The birth and its success then motivated us to create another innovation in water, which resulted in the highly innovative WaterTek Africa!

Give the readers some insight into your business?

Jamii Africa is a mobile micro health insurance product for the low income and informal sector population. What we did is built a mobile policy management platform that performs all administration activities of the insurer and then formed strategic partnerships with Jubilee Insurance and telecom companies. These enabled us to cut insurance administration costs by 95%, allowing us to launch a health insurance product starting from just $1 per month! The objective of Jamii is to reduce home births, maternal deaths and deaths from curable diseases in Africa by giving the poor population action to hospital care. In the first year alone we were able to impact lives of over 7,000 families in Tanzania.

In your opinion, what do you consider as some of the top skills needed to be a successful entrepreneur?

I believe passion is all you need and the rest is cherry on top! Passion for your idea or business is what keeps you motivated through the bad and good times; it keeps you seeking out investors, customer satisfaction and all the perseverance that you need to keep your business running.

What demographic group would you consider as your key clients?

People in Africa whose income in less than $70 per month are Jamii key clients. We call them low income and informal sector population. 80% of these are farmers, the rest are commercial motorists, house helps, street vendors and the like.

What have been some of your challenges and lessons learned from them?

One of our biggest struggles with Jamii was minimal information the target market had about insurance services, what it really means, its impact to their house hold budgets and why it is important. We were literally forced to first educate the nation broadly about financial services, then about insurance, before pitching a Jamii sale to them. A process that is costly, but again that's the downside of being a first entrant.

In today's challenging world, what do you do to stay on top of the game?

Focus on building a great product or service, and keep it great throughout! I use to worry about competition and what was happening in the market, something that kept me sleepless, worried and pulled back from actually improving my business and adding innovation to what we already had. But keeping track of 'people' only pulls you back. Stay on top of the game by focusing on having an amazing product and great customer reviews! Investing on your team and yourself by adding more skills and learning constantly is equally important.

What does success mean to you and the best way to achieve long-term success?

I have my secret magical number! The day I hit that revenue target, I would most likely stop working as hard :-)! But I'm hugely driven and I want to impact the lives of just 3 million Africans positively through technology and seeing

Jamii or waterTek taking me towards that and that is success to me. I'd say, setting a target and staying true to it is the only way to achieve long term success.

What has been your most satisfying moment in business?

Hearing positive feedback from my customers is the most satisfying moment! Hearing comments like "Jamii helped me bring my baby to the world" or "If it wasn't for Jamii I would have lost my sister," melts my heart and keeps me motivated to do more and reach more people!

How has being an entrepreneur affected your (family) life?

It has been a lot of sacrifices, something that eats my conscious daily; the late nights at work and travels…they take up 80% of my time. However, entrepreneurship has its way of giving you long breaks, which I use to make up for lost time with my husband and two beautiful daughters. On the bright side, it has really moved the family from one income class to the upper.

What other sacrifices have you made to be a successful entrepreneur?

Losing an amazing job that was really paying me well at the time; about $3,500 per month. It was a very sad moment for me, but hey!

On average, how many hours do you work per day and what is your typical day like?

I'm not a morning person, so I would start my day at 9:00 (something I have to change). I then catch up with my emails, then start with meetings during the first half of the day, then do official calls/conferences after lunch. I love spending the second half of the day in my office, uninterrupted, either finishing up work then do tons of readings over the internet, something I deeply enjoy. I close the day with daily update meetings with my Co-Founder and partners.

Where do you see yourself and business in another 10 years?

Impacting the lives of 10 million Africans through technology, Jamii or waterTek or both added together :-).

What are your guiding personal and business principles?

Every day the business must have made a step towards its vision - every single day! It could be from just one email, one conversation or a small contract or just a valuable network, but every single day there has to be a step towards the vision, and we stay true to this.

What is your greatest fear, and how do you manage fear?

I fear failure... I fear having to ever close a business or bring down my expectations or goals in life because of any realities of life. When the feeling of fear comes, I try to think of the struggles Jamii had as a start up, the initial two years of running a business off my salary and all the hurdles that came with that; and if we survived that, we will survive anything, even failure! I also pray a lot. I talk to God about the problems and achievements and He has always been there for us.

What is your best aspect of being an entrepreneur?

The awards that come with it! We have won multiple local and international awards, including being named Africa's Top women innovator 2016 by The World Economic Forum. It is so satisfying when your efforts are being acknowledged!

Do you have role models and why?

I look up to various African successful entrepreneurs. I admire and learn from aspects of each of their success stories, but I believe my end goal is my motivation and inspiration.

What are your hobbies and what do you do to relax?

I love travelling and play-time with my daughters; they get

me vexed at times, drive me crazy but crack my ribs the hardest!

Do you have any favourite quote or saying?

"Do not build a good product, build a Ferrari" Not sure where I picked that, but it has been with me from the time I was building Jamii to building waterTek. It makes me do projects at no rush, relaxed and taking my time at it, because in my heart, we are not building a product, we are building the Ferrari of health insurance, Ferrari of water system management or anything else!

What advice or message do you have for young Africans who want to become entrepreneurs?

Whenever you think of what business or side project to do, make sure it's nothing 'basic' and lastly, do something you truly love and enjoy; it will be easy!

It's better to walk alone than with a crowd going in the wrong direction.

- Diane Grant, Canadian playwright & Screenwriter

MUSTY AHMED
Aisha Investment

Musty Ahmed is the founder and Chief Executive Officer of Aisha Investment, a marketer and wholesaler of indigenous West African foods and drinks. Established in 1998 in The Netherlands, it imports various types of West African food products and redistribute them under the product line of *Fola Foods* across Europe.

The strategic location of Amsterdam gives Aisha Investment a geographic advantage in terms of transportation network in continental Europe vis-a-vis the United Kingdom. Today, Fola Foods has grown to be one of the European largest household names among retailers, consumers and high end users.

With a vision to be a leader in the distribution of made in West African food products in Europe, Ahmed says: "our products conform to the strict European laws concerning local language name, bar code, expiring date, batch code and the full description of the content. "We work in accordance with the strict European laws as regards the Hazard Analysis Critical Control Point (HACCP)."

The Interview:

How did the idea for your business come about?

I stumbled by chance into this business, starting around 1998 when African food products were expensive and what was obtainable in the market were undesirable. I saw the niche in the market to provide the numerous West Africans residing in The Netherlands good quality products at very affordable prices and since then we have grown in leaps and bounds.

Give the readers some insight into your business?

We specialise in importing various typical West African foods, provisions and drinks into Europe from Nigeria, Ghana, Cameroun and Benin Republic. Our operational centre is in Amsterdam where all the goods are warehoused and redistributed to various wholesalers and retail shops across Europe.

In your opinion, what do you consider as some of the top skills needed to be a successful entrepreneur?

In my case because I reside in The Netherlands, the Dutch language skill is a must.

What demographic group would you consider as your key clients?

It's actually hard to tell these days as even the mainstream Europeans are also consuming African foods; so I think it cut across all demographics, but certainly the majority of our clients are West Africans.

What have been some of your challenges and lessons learned from them?

The Netherlands is a very thorough country in terms of following laid down rules and regulations concerning food. As a result, we were confronted with so many Hazard Analysis Critical Control Point rules (HACCP). Compliant is a must and there are no two ways about it.

In today's challenging world, what do you do to stay on top of the game?

We have been able to wriggle around our challenges by working with experts in the field and doing the right thing before importing our products into Europe.

What does success mean to you and the best way to achieve long-term success?

Success means patience, perseverance, foresight, determination and honesty. When and if you have these ingredients cemented with the grace of God, achieving long term success is guaranteed.

What has been your most satisfying moment in business?

My most satisfying moment is when I see my clients being happy with the products we sell; it becomes a win-win situation for everybody.

How has being an entrepreneur affected your (family) life?

Unfortunately, I would love to spend more time with my family but the many business related travels do take me away. This is the most challenging aspect of being an entrepreneur.

What other sacrifices have you made to be a successful entrepreneur?

24 hours is too short for a day as you have to always be in constant touch with new regulations everywhere, new innovations and keep abreast with your competitors products. Invariable you have

to become news junkie. That keeps you also away from the little time you can have for yourself or family.

On average, how many hours do you work per day and what is your typical day like?

No day is the same; you might start the day on a quiet note and end it being exhausted, whereas another day can start being busy and end up quiet, but by and large it's a very intense venture. A minimum of 10 hours per day is ideal and sometimes we work on Saturdays too.

Where do you see yourself and business in another 10 years?

Very hard to tell, but I think we might be working more directly from Africa than in Europe. Labour and the cost of running a business in Europe is really capital intensive.

What are your guiding personal and business principles?

Be fair and honest in everything you do.

What is your greatest fear, and how do you manage fear?

My greatest fear is losing someone close to me but since it's inevitable you just keep on moving.

What is your best aspect of being an entrepreneur?

When I see the credit alerts and when clients patronise our new products.

Do you have role models and why

Yes, certainly, my parents. They laid the foundation of work ethics in me and when the time arrived to be a man it was easy to adapt.

What are your hobbies and what do you do to relax?

I'm a news junkie but certainly reading, watching movies and being around my family is always fun.

Do you have any favourite quote or saying?

Do your best and leave the rest.

What advice or message do you have for young Africans who want to become entrepreneurs?

You can be whatever you venture to be; the sky is the limit as long as you're real, honest, focus and patient, but most importantly, believe in God which may sound like a cliché, but that's the truth.

The man who moves a mountain begins by carrying away small stones.

- Confucius, Philosopher and Teacher

MWANGI KIRUBI
Click Pictureworks Africa

Mwangi Kirubi, known to many as 'Mwarv' is a successful photographer and the personality behind the lens of Click Pictureworks Africa.

Mwangi Kirubi, known to many as Mwarv says Africa is blessed and he's on a mission to show the world the beauty of the continent's diversity. He sees himself as a storyteller keen on showcasing Africa's beauty and cultures to shift perceptions from the common narrative.

Mwangi Kirubi: "Africa is a very blessed continent, but many Africans don't see it that way.

"We believed the skewed negative stories about Africa

to the point of pitying ourselves and seeking the riches of the lands from where these storytellers come. "With every click I take, I will show you what a blessed place we live in. "I'll rebrand Africa, one click at a time."

The Interview:

How did the idea for your business come about?

I didn't set out wanting to be a photographer. I just got curious about it when working as a copywriter at a local radio station. I quit that job to pursue a hobby that had become a passion and ten years later, I have no regrets.

Give the readers some insight into your business?

Using my lenses, I shed light on stories about Africans doing inspiring things, from farming to education and engineering.

In your opinion, what do you consider as some of the top skills needed to be a successful entrepreneur?

Honesty. I don't think there's any virtue that surpasses being truthful to yourself and your client. If you can't deliver on a job, don't take it on and let the client know that you can't. If you know someone who can do it better, recommend them to your client.

What demographic group would you consider as your key clients?

Most of my clients are non-profit organisations working in Africa. But my biggest client is myself, because I need to satisfy the desire to tell these stories, whether I'm being paid to do so or not.

What have been some of your challenges and lessons learned from them?

I was once detained in a police station in Uganda for half a day. I'd gone there to seek their consent to take photos in town but they suspected me of terrorism. Despite it being a setback, I took it in good spirits, laughed about it and continued with the project. I have found that laughter in the face of adversity does wonders.

In today's challenging world, what do you do to stay on top of the game?

I wouldn't consider myself to be on top of my game. To get there, I share the knowledge I have with those who have the time to learn. I also collaborate on projects with other photographers as 'iron sharpens iron'.

What does success mean to you and the best way to achieve long-term success?

Success is doing what God created me for. In that respect, I consider myself successful at the moment.

What has been your most satisfying moment in business?

I'm still amazed that my wife and daughter and I live on photography alone. It isn't something that I thought possible. But God's favour has brought clients and opportunities to make this a reality.

How has being an entrepreneur affected your (family) life?

Work-life balance is something I work on daily. I'm committed to my business and family. Both fight for my time. It's an ongoing balancing act and I need to make sure the balance is just right.

What other sacrifices have you made to be a successful entrepreneur?

I've had to decline projects because I believed I couldn't deliver in the best way possible. That meant saying no to lucrative contracts. This in turn has allowed me to concentrate on my strengths and be a man of my word.

On average, how many hours do you work per day and what is your typical day like?

No two days are alike. Though most days start with me reading 'The Word', checking email and establishing any urgent matters that need to be handled. Some entire days are spent editing photos, responding to emails and writing proposals, others are spent partly in meetings or in the field making stories through photography.

Where do you see yourself and business in another 10 years?

In the next 10 years Click Pictureworks Africa will have a network of storytellers across Africa telling stories about Africans that inspire Africans to love themselves more.

What are your guiding personal and business principles?

As stated earlier, honesty - to myself and the client.

What is your greatest fear, and how do you manage fear?

I am fearless!

What is your best aspect of being an entrepreneur?

I wouldn't trade being in control of my own time for any amount on a pay check. It is such a liberating feeling when I wake up and I know that what I do on any day is totally dependent on me and not someone in HR or any CEO.

Do you have role models and why?

I'm yet to find a role model.

What are your hobbies and what do you do to relax?

To relax, I travel out of town, pitch my tent and take more photos.

Do you have any favourite quote or saying?

'Whatever you do, work at it with all your heart as though you were working for God and not an earthly master.'

What advice or message do you have for young Africans who want to become entrepreneurs?

Going into business isn't easy. There are challenges and obstacles to be faced, but the rewards are much more than what you'll find on a pay check at the end of the month. Find what you are so passionate about that you can do it for free, then find a way of someone paying you to do it.

Success is the sum of small efforts repeated day in and day out.

- Robert Collier, American writer

OSINE & ANESI IKHIANOSIME
BluDoors Corporation

Two teenage brothers, 15-year-old Osine Ikhianosime, and 17-year-old Anesi Ikhianosime are the co-founders of BluDoors Corporation, a technology company that help users get faster web browsing speed, no matter the network connection.

BlueDoors is able to achieve this feat via its Crocodile Browser, a software application for retrieving, presenting, and traversing information resources on the World Wide Web.

While Osine who writes the code is the Chief Executive Officer, his brother, Anesi who (can also code), designs the user interface is the Chief Operating Officer. Both started learning how to self-code at age 12 and 14 respectively.

The two Nigerian teenage techies who were inspired by the Microsoft Windows platform originally launched the mobile browser on the Mobango app store before moving to Google Play Store in order to reach a wider audience. In the near future, they plan to expand into gaming and apps that will solve real social problems such as traffic and communication.

The Interview:

How did the idea for your business come about?

We were on summer holidays and got bored. We had some challenges using the mobile web on a low end android device. It was at that point that we both decided to work on a browser that would work for us.

Give the readers some insight into your business?

At BluDoors, we are focused on how we can help improve the mobile web experience for users.

In your opinion, what do you consider as some of the top skills needed to be a successful entrepreneur?

To be a successful Entrepreneur, you need to be able to take calculated risks, recognise opportunities, be confident and have great leadership skills,

What demographic group would you consider as your key clients?

Anyone that uses the internet and want a fast all-in-one experience (searching, browsing and downloading) falls within our demographic group.

What have been some of your challenges and lessons learned from them?

Our greatest challenge has been the poor internet connection in Nigeria. As a result, it has helped us to become more patient.

In today's challenging world, what do you do to stay on top of the game?

We keep learning to grow.

What does success mean to you and the best way to achieve long-term success?

We feel success is never accidental. Hard work breeds success!

What has been your most satisfying moment in business?

Our most satisfying moment in business would be when

people tell us how our product, Crocodile Browser changed their mobile browsing experience for good.

How has being an entrepreneur affected your (family) life?

Being an Entrepreneur has so far not affected our family life.

What other sacrifices have you made to be a successful entrepreneur?

We have sacrificed lots of sleep to get our business to where it is today.

On average, how many hours do you work per day and what is your typical day like?

On average we work for about 5-6 hours maximum per day and an hour extra on weekends.

Where do you see yourself and business in another 10 years?

In 10 years from now, we hope to have significantly changed the mobile browsing experience of the people that use our product(s).

What are your guiding personal and business principles?

Our guiding personal and business principle is that the best kind of motivation is self motivation. Your motivation is what drives you from inside to do great things. "Each of us is endowed with innate resources that enable us to achieve all we have ever dreamed of and more.

What is your greatest fear, and how do you manage fear?

We have never had any fear.

What is your best aspect of being an entrepreneur?

Our best aspect of being an Entrepreneur is having the freedom to explore and manage our business while still taking calculated risks.

Do you have role models and why?

Yes, we do. Mark Zuckerberg, the founder of Facebook is really inspiring.

What are your hobbies and what do you do to relax?

Osine enjoys playing the piano, soccer and learning new things. Anesi on the other hand plays soccer and enjoys learning new things as well.

Do you have any favourite quote or saying?

Difficulty is an illusion of the mind for everything is easy on a given time.

What advice or message do you have for young Africans who want to become entrepreneurs?

If you have an idea that can impact the lives of people positively, just do it. It doesn't have to be an idea that will change the world.

The only way you are going to have success is to have lots of failures first.

- Sergey Brin, Computer Scientist & Entrepreneur

PATRICIA JUMI
GrowthAfrica

Patricia Jumi is the Managing Director and co-founder of GrowthAfrica, a business that is accelerating the growth of many businesses in Africa. She's an entrepreneur at heart and very passionate about Africa, knowing that its development and most of its problems can be solved by innovative social businesses.

GrowthAfrica is a growth frontier. It focuses on growing successful enterprises in Africa through business acceleration, strategic advice and access to investments. It's the business runway to success for local businesses seeking a platform for their business take-off and for international companies in need of a market landing space and growth hub.

The Interview:

How did the idea for your business come about?

I was part of a team that was responsible for helping a Danish IT company expand into several African countries and after that I started assisting many companies that wanted to enter Africa find opportunities to invest in and also companies to partner with. Some of these partnerships involved working with over 1500 small businesses and I realised most of them are not growing and creating impact because they did not have a clear business strategy and did not know how to access investment.

Give the readers some insight into your business?

We work with early stage and growth stage businesses who want to have a financial and social impact on the customers they work with. We help them articulate their businesses better, help them double their revenue and also raise the necessary investment needed to grow and scale their businesses. For our early stage businesses, we work with them through 6-month cohort accelerator programmes.

In your opinion, what do you consider as some of the top skills needed to be a successful entrepreneur?

Understanding financials, listening and leadership. You need to understand your numbers. Listening not only to your employees but also your customers - you need to know if you are truly solving their problem or addressing their needs. Leadership especially in articulating the vision and ensuring that everyone you are working with is onboard and has taken ownership.

What demographic group would you consider as your key clients?

We don't have a particular demographic per se; most of our clients range between the ages of 26 years to even 70. For our business acceleration activities which target post revenue early stage entrepreneurs they usually fall within 26 to 45 years.

What have been some of your challenges and lessons learned from them?

Partnerships, finding the right ones have been challenging especially finding organisation that share the core key values. Lesson learned is take your time to understand your potential partner and if it not working cut it lose and don't stick out because of appearances. I go with the Mantra: take your time when seeking the right partners but bolt out fast if it is not working.

In today's challenging world, what do you do to stay on top of the game?

Reading, Reading. You have to know what is happening around you not only what your competitors are doing but what the trends are; what are the issues people are talking about. This has helped us a lot. Also we are innovation driven and so we are always tweaking our model and adapting to the different businesses we are dealing with.

What does success mean to you and the best way to achieve long-term success?

Success for me is achieving what you set out to do despite the challenges and obstacles that you face. For me this has been key and I would like to say for me it is not comparing myself to anyone but is comparing my previous record to the latest one. So I always enjoy working with goals and targets because each time I achieve them that is success and promotion for me.

What has been your most satisfying moment in business?

Seeing us launch into new countries besides Kenya. We recently launched into Uganda and Ethiopia; this has been a dream come true, but we still have to expand to several African countries, so still have work to do.

How has being an entrepreneur affected your (family) life?

In the beginning, you tend to spend all the time and thoughts on your business. You know ideas come to you in the middle of the night and most of the times you are thinking of your business and how you can get ahead of the curve and what you need to improve on etc. So you find yourself working after 5pm and on weekends. I have now learnt to find a balance and I ensure I stop discussing or thinking about work at 7pm and I also try to keep my Sundays void of work.

What other sacrifices have you made to be a successful entrepreneur?

I really wouldn't say that they are sacrifices. I look at them more like temporary things you have to give up to ensure you are meeting your goals as an organisation. Giving up weekends, holidays and extravagance to ensure that I am leaving behind an organisation that can continue creating impact and an outlier in what it does.

On average, how many hours do you work per day and what is your typical day like?

I usually put in a 12-14-hour day, but when we have workshops and crucial timelines then this will be longer and my energy will be focused on achieving the target we have set out to achieve. My day will involve meetings with different stakeholders; potential entrepreneurs, current entrepreneurs, investors, speakers etc. responding to emails, depending on the day meeting with my team and also facilitating some of the workshops we run.

Where do you see yourself and business in another 10 years?

In over 20 African countries working with entrepreneurs that are changing the status-quo in these countries.

What are your guiding personal and business principles?

Integrity, honesty and faith! Integrity - everything I do should be from a point of truth; honesty whether it is with my employees, suppliers or entrepreneurs. Faith, this is every ingredient that every entrepreneur must have because without it you cannot grow or create and conceive ideas or concepts that can be executed. Also if you have faith, you will be persistent and not give in at the first challenge. This is crucial especially since statistics keep saying that 80% of start-ups fail in their 1st year. I can't allow this to be a statistic.

What is your greatest fear, and how do you manage fear?

I have through the years dealt with fear because it brings too much anxiety; so I have focused on growing my faith through the study of the word of God but also focusing on knowing that I can do anything I set my mind to do and this is the mentality we share at GrowthAfrica. Fear attacks the mind; so we always have to ensure we listen to the right news and focus on the right thoughts and resist bad and negative thoughts from entering our minds because we are living in a world where every day you turn on the TV or read the papers everything sounds bad; the stock markets are falling, no one is investing and so on, name it. But I refuse to focus on these things and see them all as opportunities.

What is your best aspect of being an entrepreneur?

Impacting lives through your products and services. The satisfaction of knowing that you are changing lives or improving processes of businesses that change lives of people. This is fulfilling!

What are your hobbies and what do you do to relax?

I spend time with my husband, I love watching movies and reading. I am also active in church and I love travelling and seeing new places and people.

Do you have any favourite quote or saying?

Any business without a goal or target is just hallucinating and not ready to grow. Growth is planned and not mysterious as most think. Rather is it the application of revealed principles and means.

What advice or message do you have for young Africans who want to become entrepreneurs?

Go for it, find a need/opportunity that needs to be addressed and go for it. Do not be motivated by money but the desire to change things. Money will just gravitate to you if you are building your business on the right foundation. Also I know many young Africans will say that they can't get access to investment but most things it is not even money that you need in the beginning but to validate what your idea/business is all about.

Don't find fault... find a remedy.

- Henry Ford, Industrialist

PAUL MAGNUS OVIAWE
International College of Commerce

Paul Magnus Oviawe is the proprietor of International College of Commerce (ICC) based in Amsterdam, The Netherlands.

ICC was founded in 2000 as a not-for-profit company limited as is recognised by United Kingdom professional awarding organisations as an education provider in the Benelux (Belgium, Netherlands & Luxembourg) region. It introduced professional education bodies like ACCA, CIMA, CTH and ICEAW into the Benelux education market and as such, is a foremost Institution.

Originally from Warri, Delta state of Nigeria, Paul Oviawe has lived in the Netherlands for 20 years.

The Interview:

How did the idea for your business come about?

It jumps started after my experiences with Dutch Higher Education. Higher education in The Netherlands is preposterously detailed, difficult and most of all innovative. To tell you the least, I experienced countless burnouts struggling to fit into the education system. Frankly in nearly all cases it was a wall to wall encounter. But at the end I survived against all odds.

With my academic proofs in my basket, I was ready for the white collar job market, but to my surprise the job market was not ready for me or my kind at least at that time. I struggled and struggled with no success. It was against this backlash I had no other choice than to switch on my thinking cap. I brainstormed, did some market research and gathered some fellow educators and the International College of Commerce was born.

Give the readers some insight into your business?

ICC has a wide ranging professional qualification portfolio including accounting, finance, management and marketing. These qualifications are internationally recognised by employers, governments and professional bodies for delivery to regular and corporate students. More so, ICC maintains an extensive corporate-student training network with major multinational companies, which includes Adidas, Cisco, GEC, KPMG, Mitsubishi, NIKE, Shell, AERCAP and TomTom to mention a few in the region.

ICC also initiates and support educational projects with local universities in diverse parts of developing countries. We believe the role of education in poverty eradication, in close co-operation with other social sectors, is crucial to reducing poverty. Our latest project Academic Resource Centre (De ARC) is a library project supported by Dutch Universities of Maastricht, VU and Wageningen. De-ARC project is to develop a knowledge-hub that promotes reading and lifelong learning. The hub will provide access to study materials for students, teachers and researchers;

materials that will help redefine existing fundamental values and work towards concrete improvements of lives and environments in the Niger Delta region of Nigeria.

In your opinion, what do you consider as some of the top skills needed to be a successful entrepreneur?

As an African migrant, doing business in The Netherlands can be compared to swimming nude in a shark infested swimming pool; you know the clock is ticking. Everything, including your scent, smile, looks, voice and the weather is against you. That notwithstanding, to be more distinct there are two angles to address this question: On one hand the human or natural part which is simply a good knowledge of what you do; keep updating that knowledge, keep watching what your competitors are doing and above all listen to the customers or clients. On the other hand, there exist the supernatural demands, which is luck.

What demographic group would you consider as your key clients?

Every person or persons seeking professional knowledge to start or advance their careers. In today's world to be easily employed you have to have a profession or work towards one. And to retain your job you need career development. In other to survive, you have to add to your existing human capital by gaining western education.

What have been some of your challenges and lessons learned from them?

At ICC our experience is multifaceted. Our students come from different countries, academic and work backgrounds and ages. We learn a lot from their different educational experiences. A crucial part of my job is to make sure that our talented passionate tutor team regularly finds common grounds of study and make every moment enjoyable for the student.

In today's challenging world, what do you do to stay on top of the game?

We are actually not on top of the professional education delivery market. We are simply the original institute within the Benelux region. Getting the education job done for us is more interesting than struggling to be on top.

What has been your most satisfying moment in business?

Giving back to societies and individuals in need is incalculable. I might not have the financial freedom but I certainly have the ideas and connections in The Netherlands to propel a collective good. As such anytime I have the opportunity to create or be part of a collective good, I am at peace with my humanity. Our De ARC university library project is expected to support over 100.000 university students in the Niger-delta region. We Africans spend more time, energy and money with church activities than any other race. We attend to church activities and we run away from doing common good. I am convinced that human happiness comes from the smallness of improvements and in my opinion to do good is the best way to glorify God.

How has being an entrepreneur affected your (family) life?

Greatly! I am blessed with a robust African queen as a wife. She understands the primary needs of a real African man in the battlefield.

What other sacrifices have you made to be a successful entrepreneur?

Working together and sharing. I learn to share as well as to work-together for a common agenda, and that has made our business and foundation activities stronger and long lasting.

On average, how many hours do you work per day and what is your typical day like?

I have a working wife and we work together to manage each

other's working hours. For me its five hours of work per week and the rest is with my family. As a self-employed person, I have flexible working schedule.

Where do you see yourself and business in another 10 years?

ICC is not in the business of making profit but rather human advancement, so I guess and hope I will still be in the business of not-making profit and planning retirement. But as the actor Clint East wood said, "Tomorrow is promised to no one."

What are your guiding personal and business principles?

Live and let Live (Let us enjoy the pleasures and opportunities which life offers and to allow others to do the same).

What is your greatest fear, and how do you manage fear?

How to make education accessible to young learners in remote parts of Africa; to transfer education and skills to the locals to constructively develop their environment. I actually do not see any real commitment from African leaders or world bodies.

What is your best aspect of being an entrepreneur?

To see my students, laugh when they have good grades and get better jobs

Do you have role models and why?

I do not believe in role modelling. I believe everyone is just doing their thing in their own ways. I am no different.

What are your hobbies and what do you do to relax?

I am a home-body, a family man. I take joy playing with my children. Apart from family time, swimming is my favourite pastime. I now have a swimming diploma.

Do you have any favourite quote or saying?

"Take your work seriously, live modestly, love and share

generously and leave the rest to God."

What advice or message do you have for young Africans who want to become entrepreneurs?

My advice for all Africans is to start taking 'Ownership and Accountability' of your actions by taking Responsibility. Majority of us are always stalled with blaming others for our deeds in domestic or business dealings, waiting on someone else to take initiative to get things moving or hoping the other person assumes blame and fixes the issue. We always look for easy way out or quick fixes from an unexpected, diabolic or divine source.

Start where you are. Use what you have. Do what you can.

- Arthur Ashe

SAM TURYATUNGA
Tursam Investments Limited

Sam Turyatunga is the founder and Chief Executive Officer of Tursam Investments Limited, a fruit juice processing company that deals in natural fruit drinks marketed under the Brand name Uhuru Fruit Drinks in Uganda.

The 27-year-old Food Scientist received his Bachelor of Science degree in Food Processing Technology from Kyambogo University, Kampala Uganda.

The Interview:

How did the idea for your business come about?

The idea of the business started while at the university in my second year of a four year programme in 2013. Due to financial constraints as a student and looking at my family financial constraints, I decided to start a business. My 96 year-old father has 3 (three) wives, with my 66-year-old mother being the third wife. At that time, I realised that with Food processing Technology, I could start self employment and raise some money for myself as a student.

So, from my single bedroom hostel, I started buying a few pineapples, passion fruits and bananas and decided to make fresh juice from them and sell them to my fellow students using disposable cups. I would wake up very early to make fresh juice. Meanwhile, I employed some fresh university graduates who were unemployed and they would sell this juice as I attended classes for lectures.

However, it got to a point where I had the challenge of extending the shelf-life of my juices. I didn't know anything about preservation and the lifestyle of making fresh juices everyday became too hard because sometimes, these juices would go bad due to weather conditions, especially when it rains; that's when people consume less. I would have to throw away up to 40 litres of the juices, causing a big set back to my small business as a student.

So, one of our lecturers Professor G.W Bazirake Byarugaba, advised me to apply for space at one of the Agribusiness incubators in Uganda called Afribanana products limited which promotes innovations in banana value chain. I applied and I was recruited as an incubatee. They trained me in banana juice processing and preservation at their company during my industrial attachment. I did further research and I learnt how to preserve other types of fruit juices, making it possible to have a shelf life of up to 6 months. I continued this processing until I completed my university education in May of 2015 when I decided to commercialise my products.

Give the readers some insight into your business?

Our products include juices of banana, mango, pineapple and banana wine. We also do value addition to cereals and now have a new product blended from sorghum and millet. It's a malt drink, fermented but non-alcoholic cereal beverage locally known as "" Bushera", a traditional drink in Ugandan culture.

In your opinion, what do you consider as some of the top skills needed to be a successful entrepreneur?

The most important skill is patience and commitment. In my opinion, to be successful, all entrepreneurs must have these traits.

What demographic group would you consider as your key clients?

We provide nutritious and affordable products to young corporate people and middle income earners offering natural and high value content.

What have been some of your challenges and lessons learned from them?

At the beginning, I was using my dormitory room, but soon the university gave me permission to use the food laboratory to process my juices. After using the food laboratory for only 2 months, some of my lecturers didn't support my idea because I was making more money than them and they forced me to stop doing my innovations from the university premises. This was a big challenge. I later overcame that when my biological elder brother offered me space at his residence in Kampala. The experience taught me the importance of tolerance and patience and that not every one wishes you well.

Second challenge was that of operational capital. There was great demand in the market but I didn't have enough money for production. However, with my trustworthiness, family and friends helped me with some money which I would use and pay back.

Another challenge was customers' not making complete payment. I solved this by reducing the credit opportunities offered to them. I have learnt to know my clients and to identify the trustworthy and untrustworthy ones.

In today's challenging world, what do you do to stay on top of the game?

Keep innovating and finding out what the clients want; then

offering exactly that. It's better to do what they want, rather than forcing your ideas on them.

What does success mean to you and the best way to achieve long-term success?

To me success means achieving my dreams through transforming other people's lives in my community. To achieve long term success requires operating a business with the right system that are sustainable and doesn't require a specific person to run, but can be run by any other person who takes over the roles of a previous key person. Most businesses in Africa collapse because once the founder dies, the business dies. For a business to live long, the right system that is sustainable should be in place.

What has been your most satisfying moment in business?

Having my products certified by Uganda National Bureau of standards in July 2016.

What other sacrifices have you made to be a successful entrepreneur?

I have sacrificed some quick ways of making money in order to build my business into a multi- billion company. I have sacrificed long time friends who would want me to be with them in luxury but have chosen to dedicate my time towards my business.

On average, how many hours do you work per day and what is your typical day like?

On average I work 12 hours a day, with my typical day like this: wake-up at 5:30am for morning devotion//prayer and reading the Word of God//Bible; prepared for work at 6:00am: be at the factory at 7:00-8:00am to meet staff and plan for work to be done for the day. At 8:30am, I accompany our company delivery van to the field for marketing, sales and distribution of our products. At 5:00pm, I return to factory to assess the work done, meet managers at factory, including any other appointments. Go home at 6:00pm - end of my working day.

What are your guiding personal and business principles?

On a personal level, I keep company with people with a vision; and on business principles, I keep innovating for what the customer want and not what I want.

What is your greatest fear, and how do you manage fear?

Failing to achieve a certain goal; I always make sure I set goals that I have the ability to reach in order to avoid stress.

Do you have role models and why?

Yes I have. They keep me focused and motivated that at one point in life, I will get there! And even be better than them.

Do you have any favourite quote or saying?

No one in life is in charge of your happiness; you are the reason you smile!

What are your hobbies and what do you do to relax?

Social media; I go online - Facebook, Twitter, WhatsApp and I see what's trending in news headlines, on social media, in the world etc.

What is your best aspect of being an entrepreneur?

It has given me a completely different thinking towards life. I don't waste time with vision-less people. I only give time to people who value their lives too.

Where do you see yourself and business in another 10 years?

I see Tursam Investments Limited as one of East Africa's biggest processor of fruits and vegetables into various value added products.

What advice or message do you have for young Africans who want to become entrepreneurs?

Be innovative. Innovations that can transform

communities! An innovation that can't change your financial status or have any positive impact is not an innovation.

Too many people are quick to dream big, but slow to act on it.

- Edmond Mbiaka, Writer

SANGU DELLE
Golden Palm Investment

Sangu Delle is Founder and Chief Executive Officer of Golden Palm Investments (GPI), an investment holding and advisory company focused on high growth and impact industry sectors in Africa.

With its headquarters in Ghana, GPI operates companies and funds promising start-ups that can have social impact and generate jobs. It makes long-term investments in the healthcare, real estate, financial services, agri-business and technology, employing a highly disciplined approach to its operations, risk management and investments

Sangu is also the co-founder of cleanacwa, which is a nonprofit working in underdeveloped communities in Ghana to provide water and sanitation.

GPI commit resources and leverage its expertise to build businesses that will have a positive and lasting impact in Africa.

The Interview:

How did the idea for your business come about?

I started GPI in 2006. On the one hand, I have always had entrepreneurship in me since I was a little boy. While in secondary school and even when I went to U.S. on scholarship to further my education, I always looked for creative ways to do something of value and make money.

I also saw a drastic change, an evolution in Africa. I saw a growing middle class and my theory was that Africa was having an economic revolution, a slowly growing but resilient economy that would take everyone by storm.

What really crystallised it all was my experience when I started an NGO for clean water in a community in 2006. After interviewing people on what significant project was important to them, I was hoping to hear that they wanted infrastructure and something of sort. Surprised, they said, "we want jobs and economic development." It then dawn on me that these same people that I have come to help, do not want a handout but jobs and economic opportunities. I started thinking beyond what I was doing at that time, that there was an opportunity to use my entrepreneurship skills combined with my desire to make a difference in Africa. It was at that point that I thought about starting a business venture.

Give the readers some insight into your business?

We are pan-African investment company with two main groups; one is an operating company that we started ourselves or acquired. For instance, the health care business has a chain of 15 clinics and hospitals.

We also have the venture capital business which allows us to invest in the best start-ups coming out of Africa, such as mPharma in Ghana that is reducing the price of drugs drastically, SOLO Mobile, a device company focused on bringing the best consumer experience to affordable smart-phone users in Nigeria, Stawi Foods in Kenya that makes baby food, Supermarkt and the leading online grocery retailer in Nigeria. We basically provide capital and support for early stage companies to help build and scale them.

In your opinion, what do you consider as some of the top skills needed to be a successful entrepreneur?

I can tell you how one can be relatively successful in Africa, and it requires a number of things. First, you require resilience, true resilience. I'll give you an example. We started an agro-export business and made all necessary projections but we ran into problems with the rain which changed the parameter of our plan. We found out that we needed heavy duty trucks and bulldozers which raised our operating costs substantially. My first instinct was let's cut our losses and get out. However, we were resilient and decided to stay on and soon got very efficient. As a result, we were able to double our output and it turned out to be literally a business with the best return on investment that we have ever made.

Secondly, it is very important to invest in your best team to have a very strong human capital. If I give you all the money in the world and you don't have a good team to execute, the right type of middle management to be able to scale, you are going to run into problem. A combination of resilience, the right vision and human capital equips you to do very well in this market.

Lastly, you have to be very innovative. Africa is not like the U.S. or Europe, where you have the right infrastructure and all that. You have to think outside the box. Adjust and adapt to the diverse business changes in the environment.

What demographic group would you consider as your key clients?

Our target and focus is the middle and working class.

What have been some of your challenges and lessons learned from them?

We have lots of challenges. One is at a micro level for instance with the issues of depreciation in different markets in Africa. Such setbacks can be quite difficult and you have to be innovative. It means that if you have extra cash, you change it into dollars to mitigate the impact. It also means that you have to rebalance the portfolio so that you can go into other sectors to help you earn enough for export.

What does success mean to you and the best way to achieve long-term success?

At the highest broadest level, success for me would be when we in Africa and our grand children in the future can look us in the eyes and say, is it true that Africa used to be poor? That they cannot believe it! That is when as a continent, I know we have succeeded.

What has been your most satisfying moment in business?

For me it's when I see the companies we help incubate scale and achieve their goals. For instance, with mPharma, we have been able to reduce the price of the medicine by 50% in Nigeria, Ghana, Gambia and Ivory Coast. When I see the social impact of our businesses on the consumers, it's the most rewarding thing for me as an entrepreneur.

How has being an entrepreneur affected your (family) life?

When I started the business, I went out to recruit my brothers to work with me. It's not by accident that the Sawiris, the billionaires in Egypt are all brothers. Look at Dangote in Nigeria who has his family members on board. You have to work with the people you trust the most. We do not have the structure and infrastructure yet in Africa to monitor everything. The most important investment is the human capital and for me, I consider it a competitive advantage by having the most trusted people around me who

I know will protect and look after my best interest.

What other sacrifices have you made to be a successful entrepreneur?

There are lots of them. Early on in the business to keep things going, I had to take 30 thousand dollars from my credit card. With business challenges, my account was down to only few thousand dollars and my assistant called me up that in two weeks we have a bill of 40 thousand dollars to pay. It has not been easy at all, but this is business and you have to face those challenges and look for solutions and become stronger

On average, how many hours do you work per day and what is your typical day like?

I start at about 6.30 am and I'm mostly in the office at 7 a.m. I usually work till midnight every day, including weekends. It's my life! As the CEO of the company, I cannot run away from my work and if I do where do I run to? If issues come up, it's on my shoulder and not on anyone else!

Where do you see yourself and business in another 10 years?

We want to be able to build a billion dollar portfolio on social and other aspects of our business that would transform the continent. We would have made significant stride towards our goals to expand a net value asset of our portfolio. mPharma will hopefully be in 20 African countries and be able to create thousands of jobs and have meaningful impact on the lives of our target group.

What are your guiding personal and business principles?

I believe in a serving leadership. One of my favourite parts of the scripture is when Jesus Christ washes the feet of the disciples, which is a different perspective on leadership. If Jesus could kneel down and do so, who are you then? I'm not just a boss but a servant to my people and it's my job to serve. That's also how I can get the best out of those who work under me. There's also the value of hard work impacted on me by my mother. I cannot control what challenges would arise at my job, but I can control my work ethics and integrity. It's important to do the right thing despite all pressures that may come your way. It has taken me 30 years to get here and it can collapse in seconds through bad ethics. So, I always make sure we are above board.

What is your greatest fear, and how do you manage fear?

My greatest fear is hubris; a Greek word which means over confidence or foolish pride. There is no greater killer than hubris and I fear it. If you have success and things are working out well and you belief you are invincible, that's the beginning of your down fall.

What is your best aspect of being an entrepreneur?

It's been extremely fulfilling to be able to caste my own destiny. As the CEO, it's challenging but you control so many aspect of the operations. It's really rewarding and extraordinarily fulfilling and I won't trade it for anything else.

Do you have role models and why?

My mother is definitely one of them. A generous and one of the most hardworking women I've ever known. She also taught me the value of hard work and understanding your privilege and knowing that whatever situation you find yourself, someone else is worse off. Anyone below you can come up as well. I have always been inspired by Kwame Nkrumah, the father of Pan African and first President of Ghana. During the independence of Ghana, he said that its independence is meaningless without the independence of the rest of Africa and I'm inspired by that vision. I have also been inspired by the like of Aliko Dangote who has built a massive enterprise in Africa, employing thousands of people. He's truly an African giant and young Africans can look at him and say I can be like him.

What are your hobbies and what do you do to relax?

I have hiked mountain Kilimanjaro and mountain Everest, I have gone paragliding off the mountain in Cape Town, I have sky dived etc. I'm an adrenalin junky!

Do you have any favourite quote or saying?

There are actually two of them and they are both spiritual in nature. The first one is from the Bible (1Timothy 4:12): Don't let anyone look down on you because you are young, but set an example for the believers in speech, in conduct, in love, in faith and in purity. The second one is hanging in my office and it's from mother Theresa: People are often unreasonable, irrational, and self-centred; forgive them anyway. If you are kind, people may accuse you of selfish, ulterior motives; be kind anyway. If you are successful, you will win some unfaithful friends and some genuine enemies; succeed anyway. If you are honest and sincere people may deceive you; be honest and sincere anyway. What you spend years creating, others could destroy overnight; create anyway. If you find serenity and happiness, some may be jealous; be happy anyway. The good you do today, will often be forgotten; do good anyway. Give the best you have, and it will never be enough; give your best anyway. In the final analysis, it is between you and God. It was never between you and them anyway!

What advice or message do you have for young Africans who want to become entrepreneurs?

Don't let anyone hold down your dreams and do not be apologetic about your dreams. Do not dream small but dream big, very big. However know that big ideas alone never make a difference, it's the execution. You have to be prepared to do the hard work it takes, think how do I actually turn my bold idea into reality, on a small scale and then scale it up. Finally, give back to the society. Start today; don't always be a taker, be a giver because it's a giver that will always receive. No matter how small, give something to help others. Don't wait until you become rich or a millionaire!

What we think, or what we know, or what we believe is, in the end, of little consequence. The only consequence is what we do.

- John Ruskin, British art critic, writer and philanthropist

SESINAM DAGADU
tinyDAVID Limited

Sesinam Dagadu is founder and CTO of tinyDAVID Limited, a small technology outfit aiming to tackle the big problems with tiny solutions in the developing world.

tinyDAVID believe that mobile technology is a very strong tool that can be used for the benefit of all no matter the social status. Its projects aim at improving the addressing system in developing countries by providing an advance, yet robust and easy way to use mobile technology for all.

Ses, as he's popularly known is best described as an accidental entrepreneur who has gained experience over the years at Harris Watson Holdings, International Automotive Research Centre, Digital & Electronic Forensic Service with U.K Metropolitan Police and Ecobank.

It was during his time at Ecobank that the problem of poor addressing system caught his attention, and when he returned abroad to complete his degree, he started working on a solution.

Ses is a system engineer who holds MEng Engineering with Business Management from Warwick University.

The Interview:

How did the idea for your business come about?

I was with the marketing team of one of the leading banks and had a bad experience when prospecting for clients. It was quiet ridiculous the amount of time we spent looking for the people. For the entire day we could meet only two customers on the average, which seemed very inefficient. Thus the idea of being a tech entrepreneur was born amidst this event and some others such as helping a friend of mine practice his naval targeting exams and seeing a hawker use a phone. I therefore dedicated much time to develop a system which is solving the problem of lack of addresses in developing countries like Ghana.

Give the readers some insight into your business?

SnooCode is the answer to the problem of lack of addresses in huge swathes of the developing world. The SnooCode system with the aid of a smart phone generates a unique alphanumeric code that you can share privately with friends or people who render services to you (e.g. food delivery, courier services and emergency service providers such as the police and ambulance services). It has been designed to be used by people of all levels of the socioeconomic ladder.

In your opinion, what do you consider as some of the top skills needed to be a successful entrepreneur?

A successful entrepreneur should be resilient, have problem solving ability to solve complex issues, have good networking skills, be efficient in his productive process by putting a system in place and have the ability to raise and manage money.

What demographic group would you consider as your key clients?

The system makes any individual, no matter their economic status, geographic location or social standing gain access to commercial and emergency services they previously could not access because they lacked a workable address.

What have been some of your challenges and lessons learned from them?

Challenges: Creating an addressing system that was robust enough to factor different phonetics and ethnical dialects; how different people interacted with the user interface and how users were being conscious about been tracked.

Lessons: It helped in developing a system that was resilient enough to detect errors; developing a system which required a low literacy level, i.e. knowing alphabets and numbers; having a system which vouches for your privacy, and developing a system which does not require any network or internet to function.

In today's challenging world, what do you do to stay on top of the game?

You need to address the need of the customer. A lot of time the customer knows the problem but does not have the solution. Don't solve the problem to impress other engineers; solve it in a way that fits the customer's way of life. As much as possible the customer should not have to learn any new skill in order to have the benefit of your innovation.

What does success mean to you and the best way to achieve long-term success?

Success means finding a solution that makes a difference to the most number of people; a solution that levels the same field for the poor and the rich, the well educated and uneducated.

What has been your most satisfying moment in business?

So far, it's been starting a programme with the Ghana National Ambulance Service that will enable 4.2 million people in the city of Accra to have access to emergency services even if they live in slumps which are unplanned with no street names or house numbers.

How has being an entrepreneur affected your (family) life?

Well, it has made it non-existent but I'm working hard to change that.

What other sacrifices have you made to be a successful entrepreneur?

Apart from taking a massive pay cut, I've moved away from a career that was very satisfying in forensics and I've relocated countries.

On average, how many hours do you work per day and what is your typical day like?

It is about 16 hours. I spend my evenings programming and spend the day trying to manage and build the businesses that have arisen out of my effort.

Where do you see yourself and business in another 10 years?

I envision myself as managing a global enterprise born in Africa that has been able to develop digital solutions to the most basic of challenges that has plagued the over 4 billion people in the developing world. Within the same time span, I envision the business as market player bringing tiny, but essential, solutions to the enormous challenges in the developing world for the affluent and less affluent, educated and the uneducated.

What are your guiding personal and business principles?

I believe that we are all here, no matter your status to solve problems and make new things possible.

What is your greatest fear, and how do you manage fear?

My greatest fear is not delivering for the people that I want to deliver to. Manage it by continuously checking to make sure we meet our KPIs and objectives.

What is your best aspect of being an entrepreneur?

You have a lot of control on what you do and when you do it. You get to learn and solve different problems on daily basis.

Do you have role models and why?

Yes, people like Kwame Nkrumah, Nikola Tesla, Henry Ford, Elon Musk. The reason being that no matter how difficult things were during their time, the world is better due to their efforts.

What are your hobbies and what do you do to relax?

Photography and relaxing by playing around with new technologies.

Do you have any favourite quote or saying?

Never let progress go ahead of understanding.

What advice or message do you have for young Africans who want to become entrepreneurs?

Always build a prototype. There is a lot of money around but nobody is willing to risk that money on someone who is not willing to put their own money, time and effort on the line. You have to happen in the game!

We only become what we are by the radical and deep-seated refusal of that which others have made of us.

- Jean-Paul Sartre, Philosopher and Writer

SIKI KIGONGO
Amagara Skincare

Siki Kigongo is the Chief Executive Officer of Amagara Skincare, the first ethical luxury skincare range formulated and produced in Uganda.

Siki who has always had a passion for international development, especially within the African continent, earned her undergraduate degree in International Media and Communications at the University of Nottingham; and an MSc in Communications (Political and Strategic Communications) at the London School of Economics. She has worked at a multitude of organisations ranging from the NRC (Norwegian Refugee Council) to UNAIDS.

Her keen interest in beauty and skincare led her to seek for ways to combine her background in development to the idea of creating a product that would assist in the efforts to empower locals to become self sustainable.

The Interview:

How did the idea for your business come about?

Following my return to Uganda, I soon came to realise that natural skincare and organic products are almost non-existent in the region. The only affordable range of skincare products available were packed with synthetic ingredients, cheap fillers and animal by-products. Not only are these harmful to the individual's skin, but also to users' health.

Whilst synthetic products still dominate the market, consumers in mature markets are increasingly purchasing beauty products containing natural ingredients. In my pursuit of such products, I came to the realisation that importing these products to our region was not only unaffordable for the larger population here, but it posed a bigger question; WHY DOES IT COST SO MUCH WHEN THE RAW MATERIALS ARE GROWN HERE?

Over 60% of the natural elements can be found right here in our own back yard; "so there seemed to be no reason why we were breaking an arm and a leg to purchase something foreign and we have the capabilities to produce it here. Sounded like a raw deal to us."

After several months and years of lab tests at the Uganda Industrial Research Institute (UIRI) Amagara Skincare was born.

Give the readers some insight into your business?

Amagara is a word borrowed from African dialect to mean life. We believe our natural skin care range should breathe new life into our clients' skin. Our Products are enriched with 100% natural extracts from fruits, vegetables & other plant materials that are all sourced from Ugandan farmers. These include Shea butter, Avocado oil, Cucumbers, Carrots, Vanilla, and Papaya, amongst others. Our collection includes Bath and Shower Gels, Hand and Body Lotions Product.

What have been some of your challenges and lessons learned from them?

As with all entrepreneurial ventures, one of the biggest challenges is the risk itself. Moving from a straightforward career path to dealing with the unknown. The fear of the unknown is one of the biggest challenges that I am constantly forced to face; job stability, the flux in your long-term plans that are dependent on new developments. Dealing with this volatility is one of the hardest parts of emerging as a new entrepreneur, although it's important to work through these moments of self-doubt, especially when you believe in your product. All business owners share these concerns I'm sure. However I've always taken the challenge within my stride, as I believe in order to have massive success, you will face massive failure.

What does success mean to you and the best way to achieve long-term success?

To me, success is multi-tiered. On one level, I would define it as being able to build a product with integrity, one that I believe in and one that adds value to the market and has a broader social impact. I want people to see my brand and respect what it stands for. Financial goals aside, nothing compares to gaining the respect of clients and professional counterparts.

In order for success to be achieved, I feel that one has to constantly have the courage to question themselves, their business, and their goals and make decisions regardless of the fear of failure. I once read that success is risk without fear, and I fully believe that.

In today's challenging world, what do you do to stay on top of the game?

By 2018, the industry estimates that global demand for natural and organic skincare will reach $13.2 billion. It's an industry that is constantly evolving, especially within virgin markets like Uganda. In Uganda alone, the personal and beauty care sales grew at a value of 16% over 2008 to 2014 and reached $210 million. As Uganda's first and only natural skincare line we are ahead although we refuse to be complacent. We regularly compare ourselves with international brands in order to make sure we are constantly striving. We pride ourselves on bringing international standards but produced locally. Our formulas are evolving to enhance the efficacy of active ingredients.

Where do you see yourself and business in another 10 years?

To be recognised as a leading brand not only within Uganda, but within Africa is something that we hope to achieve. Having been featured in "CNN's African Start Ups" to "How We Made It in Africa," it's a clear indicator that we are heading in the right direction.

They say that the success of a business is dependent on the visionary behind it, and my vision is crystal clear: Amagara Skincare will become Africa's premier natural skincare brand, and will remain a pioneer not only in Uganda but regionally. Of that I have no doubt.

What is your best aspect of being an entrepreneur?

Being an entrepreneur to me means sacrifice. Whilst it gives you an opportunity to make a mark on the world, there's a price to pay.

What is your typical day like?

A lot of the work falls on my lap and my day can see me going from overseeing a production line, to meeting a distributor in the afternoon and making deliveries in the evenings to hotels or supermarkets. There are so many aspects to a business and with a small workforce; I'm forced to fill in several roles. I sacrifice a hands-on relationship to my trade.

How has being an entrepreneur affected your (family) life?

This means that it is almost inevitable that the stresses of this venture will affect everything I do, especially my social and family life. However, I'm grateful to have a supportive family; two members of which are invested in this company itself. The support they provide, alongside those of my friends is a refuge in bad times and a place of celebration in the good.

What advice or message do you have for young Africans who want to become entrepreneurs?

My advice will revolve around 3 pillars that I always keep in mind: Patience, Perseverance and Motivation. One must have the patience to envision an end goal and see it through to completion. From our early days of incubation to producing a finished product took us several years, but from beginning in a laboratory to seeing our product on a supermarket stall is one of the greatest feelings in the world. But it would never have happened without patience. Challenges are almost guaranteed but if it's not worth fighting for, you're in the wrong business. One needs to work hard in silence, and let your success be your noise. In order for that to happen, one needs to stay motivated. Entrepreneurial success is far from easy to achieve, and many people will be discouraged by family and friends from giving up a stable salary to follow an entrepreneurial vision. I'm not saying one should be ignorant of the risks involved, but one needs to be brave. People never understand your journey because it is not theirs to understand; it is simply yours. After all, Rome wasn't built in a day.

For 37 years I've practiced 14 hours a day, and now they call me a genius.

- Pablo de Sarasate

TAOFICK OKOYA
Fico Solutions Limited

Taofick Okoya is the Chief Executive Officer of Fico Solutions Limited, a manufacturer and exporter of African related dolls and books.

Born and raised in Lagos, Nigeria, he earned a pre-degree certificate from Yaba College of Technology in Lagos before adding a Higher National Diploma in Ceramic Designs from North Staffordshire Polytechnic in United Kingdom.

Prior to starting Fico Solutions Limited, he acquired a wealth of experience working in various management positions, starting as a management trainee at Eleganza Industries, one of the biggest home-grown conglomerates in Nigeria. He later served in other capacities with the company from Sales/Marketing Manager to the level of Executive Director.

Taofick Okoya who is now constantly referred to as "the doll-maker who outsells Barbie in Nigeria" said: I have always had a great appreciation for art in its various forms and have nurtured this passion especially behind the scene in fashion.

The Interview:

How did the idea for your business come about?

I conceived the idea when I went birthday shopping for my niece and wanted to get her something that would be meaningful and also help with her development. I saw various dolls on display, and tried to rationalise how that would be of help to her development. At that point I thought if they had black dolls that she could relate with or identify with, it would have positive impact on her. That stayed on my mind and I started paying attention to availability of black dolls, and realised that there were none. My daughter was 3 at the time and she had asked me randomly "what colour am I?" realising where that may be leading to, in an upbeat and excitement, I told her she is Black. She had a sad look and I enquired why, she said she wished she was white. This I believe stemmed from all her favourite characters being white and having imagined herself in their likeness, and not seeing that image of her in the mirror.

This further drove my passion to create a doll that she and other African children can see themselves in and relate to. That was the beginning of the Queens of Africa dolls. The goal is not just selling pieces of molded plastic, but to inspire and create a sense of appreciation of them by promoting value, culture and a heritage.

Give the readers some insight into your business?

Fico Solutions Limited is the creator of the first ever Nigerian fashion doll called "The Queens of Africa" which is an arm of the Queens of Africa project which aims to empower the Nigerian/African girl child. A series of children books and inspiring music have been published and produced under the project, all geared towards the positive impact on the African/Nigerian girl child for a brighter future which has gained grounds both locally and internationally.

Fico Solutions Limited has varied and relative experiences in product manufacturing and services, which includes Toys, Promotional Products, Space Management/Design and Events Planning/Logistics.

In your opinion, what do you consider as some of the top skills needed to be a successful entrepreneur?

These includes but not limited to the following: Creativity; Accountability; Clear vision; Communication and Doggedness

What demographic group would you consider as your key clients?

Our goal is to be a globally recognised company with outlets for our products all over the world. At the moment we enjoy great acceptance from Nigeria, United States, London, France, Senegal and Canada. We have a lot of love from Brazil, and in the process of working out logistics of getting our products there.

What have been some of your challenges and lessons learned from them?

Initially, we faced acceptance issues, being the first company to embark on African inspired dolls after so many generations of predominantly white dolls. Then we had some production issues, from cost, to meeting up with demand. We also had distribution challenges as doing cross border business requires due diligence.

Currently, it's marketing and brand positioning in order to reach a great number of potential buyers in the world.

In today's challenging world, what do you do to stay on top of the game?

In today's fast and sensitive world, there is almost no room for a second chance; you get it wrong the backlash is quick and public. Creativity and innovation is key. Always keep it fresh and be in tune with the pulse of the public and time. What works now maybe obsolete in the next hour. I put myself in the position of the consumer and try to anticipate their needs/likes. You need to care about your end user. Its business UNUSUAL!

What does success mean to you and the best way to achieve long-term success?

The amount of people I am able to impact positively while providing a service/product. This is the driving force behind my concept and the business I'm engaged in.

What has been your most satisfying moment in business?

While grocery shopping in a store in Nigeria, I noticed a mother and her daughter aged about 6 years old talking and looking at me. At first I felt a bit uneasy and thought "what can they possibly be looking at me for? The girl later walked up to me and said: "I have your doll and I like her!" I almost passed out. After I regained myself I almost lifted her up and swung her around, but I was mindful of her mother. At that moment I had forgotten my role as a doll manufacturer and thought they had me mistaken for someone else they knew. It was humbling to be reminded that the reason I started QoA is a valid one. I also received an email from a parent of a bi-racial child, who expressed great joy that finally her daughter had a doll that captured her likeness. It was a touching moment for them, which in turn made it a touching moment for me.

How has being an entrepreneur affected your (family) life?

My work has had a positive impact on my family. My desire, inspiration and drive come from my family values. The success of my work is shared by all as we take family holidays where we spend quality time together. My work time and schedule is flexible so when the kids are on holiday I take a holiday too.

What other sacrifices have you made to be a successful entrepreneur?

Sacrifices I have made are ones that have been worth it thus far. These include a moderate lifestyle. I am quite conscious about how much I spend on myself, in other words, I am quite prudent when it comes to things that has to do with me personally and my comfort.

On average, how many hours do you work per day and what is your typical day like?

Work hours have become so seamless, starting right on my bed from 6 a.m. On the average I put in about 10-12 hours a day.

Where do you see yourself and business in another 10 years?

Not active in day to day activities but working to continuously seek avenues of positive impartation of the business on the new generation. That said, I do enjoy travelling and learning about people and their cultures; so that will make up for say 40% of my time by then.

What are your guiding personal and business principles?

My personal guiding principles includes 'not keeping up with the Jones'. On the business front, a lot of people will try to push various advices, suggestions or opinion on me, but ultimately the final decision and responsibility is MINE!

What is your greatest fear, and how do you manage fear?

My greatest fear at this moment would be losing our core vision to sales. There is also the fear of losing relevance in this fast pace world. I deal with fear by not focusing on the worst case scenario at any point in time; rather the possibilities that each situation offers.

What is your best aspect of being an entrepreneur?

I have never really enjoyed being a conformist. I like to think outside the box and commit to ideas I have conviction on. So being an entrepreneur gives me the freedom to exercise my creativity even when everyone else don't see or agree with me.

Do you have role models and why?

My role models change from time to time. There are different facets to everybody depending on the time and circumstance. My current champion role model is Barack Obama. He is highly intelligent, a great intellectual and quite articulate.

What are your hobbies and what do you do to relax?

I enjoy listening to music and watching documentaries to relax. I do enjoy travelling and learning about people and their culture. I also like walking and exercising in general.

Do you have any favourite quote or saying?

'If you are not willing to learn, no one can help you. If you are determined to learn, no one can stop you!' - Zig Ziglar

What advice or message do you have for young Africans who want to become entrepreneurs?

My advice: Don't go into entrepreneurship because you want to be your own boss. Ensure to have at least 5 years working experience in an established organisation; be focused and have determination; have mentors you can discuss with on a regular basis; be accountable and document your activities and success doesn't come overnight, you work towards it.

The first step toward success is taken when you refuse to be a captive of the environment in which you first find yourself.

-   Mark Caine, writer

TIGUIDANKE MOUNIR CAMARA
Tigui Mining Group

Tiguidanke Mounir Camara, a native of Guinea and former international model is the founder, Chairman & Chief Executive Officer of Tigui Mining Group, a mineral exploration company focusing on gold and diamonds in West Africa.

Her professional journey is a unique one because her career spans various industries. She has a background in fashion; was a former model and now a mining entrepreneur. Today, she is the only woman mine owner in Guinea and one of the few and youngest women mining executives across the continent.

Through partnerships and alliances, Tigui Mining Group plays a strategic role in acquiring and developing enterprises that have economic value and potential for future growth. TMG is a conglomerate of natural resources with highly experienced and competent professionals and vast knowledge in relative fields and a strong local presence with great understanding of government laws and of its local communities.

The Interview:

How did the idea for your business come about?

I have always been interested in mining. I grew up learning about it because, as you probably know, it is the major industry in my country. When modelling, I befriended jewellers who bought their gems in Africa. That got me thinking. I firmly believe that the exploitation of mineral resources is one of the key drivers for the economic development of the continent. As an African myself, I decided to get involved. I also noticed the lack of women and native involvement in mining. After the birth of my twins, I started my first mining company Camara Diamond & Gold Trading Network (CDGTN) in 2008. CDGTN is now TMG subsidiary in Guinea. Mining is different from other businesses because growth is a slow process. In this industry, you have to take a long-term view with a minimum of 10 years.

Give the readers some insight into your business?

Tigui Mining Group is a holding company. We focus on the exploitation and exploration of gold, diamonds and associated minerals in West Africa. As of today, TMG employs about 50 people, most of them are locals.

In Guinea, TMG's subsidiary, Camara Diamond & Gold Trading Network (CDGTN), has acquired mining assets totalling 356km2, valued at approximately 4 Million USD, in highly prospective regions. We own five semi-industrial gold exploitation licenses in Siguiri, and 3 diamond exploration licenses in Kerouane-Macenta. TMG has also launched a subsidiary in Côte d'Ivoire recently, and is developing a gold exploration project in partnership with a local cooperative.

TMG is one of the few woman-owned mining companies. We focus on sustainability and gender empowerment through the promotion of economic opportunities for women in our areas of exploration. We develop Agromine, a programme to empower women with sustainable agriculture opportunities, and to build community resilience. TMG strategically partners with agriculture companies to provide training courses on food hygiene, food security and income generation. The goal is to help them acquire financial independence. Women are the pillar of our economy.

In your opinion, what do you consider as some of the top skills needed to be a successful entrepreneur?

Tenacity, confidence and patience are key. Whatever industry you are in, you will experience some challenges. What makes the difference is how you react to these challenges. Passion is important too because at the end of the day, you have to love what you are doing.

What have been some of your challenges and lessons learned from them?

As a woman, it is true that I experienced discrimination in business, as mining is a male-dominated industry. But it has also worked to my benefit as I stick out in this sector. I had to work hard to prove that I am an equal business partner and I made it. I learned not to give up. The biggest challenge however has been raising funds. I created my mining company when the economic climate was still challenging. Guinea was in transition, emerging from a military coup and evolving into a democratic government. So there was a lot of instability.

How has being an entrepreneur affected your (family) life?

I wonder if you would you ask a male entrepreneur this same question …

What other sacrifices have you made to be a successful entrepreneur?

Being an entrepreneur is part of my life. It is my passion and this is what I love to do and I do not see it in terms of sacrifice. I have worked hard and adapt my lifestyle around the professional obligations such as travelling. I wouldn't change it for anything.

Where do you see yourself and business in another 10 years?

I want TMG to become a multinational corporation involved in various industries such as oil, aviation, agriculture and real estate. We are already working on it. TMG must be a key African player for the communities, benefiting the locals and being a source of sustainable development.

What are your guiding personal and business principles?

I do not give up and I give back. Integrity in business is important. I cannot consider my company successful without making a positive social impact. This is the reason why TMG represents the new generation of mining. The locals are not to be left behind. I am considered a daughter in the villages near our mining assets. I know what our needs are and I feel it is my duty to develop our resources for the benefit of our communities.

What is your favourite aspect of being an entrepreneur?

The freedom to make decisions you believe are right and the pride in seeing your ideas becoming viable economic ventures.

Do you have role models and why?

My primary role models have been and still are my parents who have always been very dynamic, progressive and ahead of their time. My mother is an entrepreneur and my father a politician. They have inspired me by teaching me to be creative and independent.

What are your hobbies and what do you do to relax?

I relax by watching a movie, reading a book or socializing. I like to go out with my friends for dinner or go dancing sometimes.

What advice or message do you have for young Africans who want to become entrepreneurs?

Start now and spend a lot of time on the ground, in the field. Be it in mining or in any other industry. The best way to learn and improve is by practicing.

He who is not conquering some fear everyday has not learned the secret of life.

   - Ralph Waldo Emerson

WYCLIFFE WAWERU MAINA
Play Guru

Wycliffe Waweru Maina, a young Kenyan entrepreneur seeks to restore the order to sustainable development - Planet, People and Profit. He's a sports junkie and a fun loving, people person who seeks to illuminate the best in everyone.

Wycliffe knows how essential bicycles are to the rural communities with low incomes and no paved roads. He also knows that the expensive imported bicycles are not affordable to these same people. It was therefore understandable that he could combine his hobby and passion for bicycles with the need of the people to make it his mission to set up the country's first bicycle assembly plant.

The Interview:

How did the idea for your business come about?

Bicycles and the Shimano brand have been common placed motivators for fun since my early childhood. We flipped willies and jumped off ramps with BMXes while the rest of the kids in the block played board games.

The hobby grew to a level where I had 6 personal mountain bikes that I barely rode as I worked as a management trainee. All this changed when I never played at all for almost a year; then I decided to turn in my resignation. The rest as they say is history. I knew what I loved (bicycles and extreme sports) but had no idea how to turn it into a business. I prayed for days and as faith would have it, I started selling second hand bicycles by the roadside. From a roadside executive I grew into writing a concept paper - growth.

Give the readers some insight into your business?

I sold bicycles while still organising specialised sporting and riding events. All the combined operations slowly mutated into thinking of how I needed to setup my own bicycle brand. It has been an everyday smaller efforts and strides which have culminated into my current position.

In your opinion, what do you consider as some of the top skills needed to be a successful entrepreneur?

Faith is all you need to be a successful entrepreneur as your WHY needs to be constantly bigger than anything that challenges you. Faith will have you believe in God and his infinite ability to make things work out for you.

What demographic group would you consider as your key clients?

The bottom of the pyramid - common everyday hard working, low income earning Africans who walk to work for hours. This demographic represents the niche for our mass market bicycles due to the domino effect presented by their empowerment while the middle income and affluent Africans are our retail clients.

What have been some of your challenges and lessons learned from them?

Low capacity - need to constantly innovate and have partners to match my growth.
Redundancy - keep learning and meeting new people to counter it.
Mentorship - growing with my network and not for it.

In today's challenging world, what do you do to stay on top of the game?

I read and pray more than I talk - faith and knowledge investments that always manifest in the physical realm.

What does success mean to you and the best way to achieve long-term success?

To me it translates to creating value in everyday life that supersedes your lifetime - inspiring others to be greater than basic. The only way to achieve this is a selfless business model that creates more value for the environment and people over your brand. All these while addressing specific societal issues that are degrading to the environment's conservation.

What has been your most satisfying moment in business?

The day I started - it was a bold step that changed my life forever. I never saw myself being that humble neither did I ever imagine waking up to a roadside setup. This was the most satisfying as it opened up a new world to me.

How has being an entrepreneur affected your (family) life?

It has strained my relations and increased the fall-out rate. Reason being that I only have two hands and two eyes which translates to only having two priorities. On a larger scale it's been great as the same Nay Sayers now see and appreciate that there was need for me to focus on building the brand over socialising. The craziest sacrifices have been the life moments missed over business engagements - weddings, funerals et al.

What other sacrifices have you made to be a successful entrepreneur?

Reducing my interaction circles to a value chain that is purely focused on growth. I had to leave networks that were not in alignment with my dreams and values after years of investing time in them.

On average, how many hours do you work per day and what is your typical day like?

I work all day, everyday - brain always engaged on the grind. But for physically dedicated input, I work for 14 hours a day. At the moment all efforts are geared on the setup of the bicycle assembly line and the national riding circuits. You would imagine that implementation should be easier than conceptualizing, but the latter actually is. The biggest challenge right now is how to expand the value chain to accommodate more knowledge transfer. This knowledge is what the proactive youth will use to create wealth, thus why it's key for sustainability of all we do.

Where do you see yourself and business in another 10 years?

Running a replicated version of the Kenyan chapter to more than 10 African states. Being a home brand for sustainable social enterprises incubation for the triple bottom line growth (Social, Environmental and Economic). I seriously hope to be alive.

What are your guiding personal and business principles?

On a personal level, I seek to inspire and reach out to one person every day. This way my impact record grows as I grow. In business, it's always been efficiency - seeking a way to always do more with less.

What is your greatest fear, and how do you manage fear?

Complacency and Procrastination! I manage it by always growing the reason why I do what I do. This way I shall always be levels above my challenges. Secondly, I hang around action led dreamers and this has helped in re-energizing me for greatness all through.

What is your best aspect of being an entrepreneur?

Growth - anyone's limited by their own imagination and not external factors.

Do you have role models and why?

I do have them for one reason - benchmarking. They constantly remind me of the need to be diligent in everyday life and its reflection to the end result.

What are your hobbies and what do you do to relax?

I read, run, cycle, play scrabble and listen to good music. I haven't been active on TV for 4 years now but I love the effect music has when fused with the theatre in our heads.

Do you have any favourite quote or saying?

Yes. "Everybody dies but not everybody lives" - Nicki Minaj.

What advice or message do you have for young Africans who want to become entrepreneurs?

First, learn to put pen on paper early even if the idea sounds very good - always seek to write it down and break it into smaller manageable tasks. Second, there are only two kinds of people in this world - ducks and eagles (seek to know your stand - birds of a feather flock together).

You're going to fall down, but the world doesn't care how many times you fall down, as long as it's one fewer than the number of times you get back up.

- Aaron Sorkin

YOHANIS GEBREYESUS HAILEMARIAM
Culinary & Lifestyle Solutions

Yohanis Gebreyesus Hailemariam, a globally trained chef with a French culinary base is the founder and host of Chef Yohanis Culinary & Lifestyle solutions.

Yohanis holds a Bachelor's degree in Fine Arts from Université Jean Monnet Saint-Etienne (France); Bachelor's degree in Gastronomy and Restaurant Management from Institut paul Bocuse (France) and a Master's degree in Psychology from the University of Phoenix, USA.

The Interview:

How did the idea for your business come about?

When I was working at the St Regis in California, I had the opportunity to watch several culinary shows during staff lunch hours. Several of the shows were on a culinary and especially on the concept aspect. I was inspired by them to come up with Chef Yohanis Culinary and Lifestyle TV show that focuses on the discovery of Ethiopian Culinary Jewels and thrive to slowly discover what the African continent has to offer.

Give the readers some insight into your business?

Chef Yohanis Brand is a healthy lifestyle brand dedicated to make the taste and health benefits of Ethiopian and more broadly of African food globally available through international products that people are used to cooking and eating. With an integrated and holistic approach, Chef Yohanis lifestyle solutions combine international food and Ethiopia's deeply rooted culinary art to promote healthy eating inspired from African produce.

In this perspective, Chef Yohnais brand has 3 distinct yet complementary approaches:
Chef Yohanis Culinary & Lifestyle TV show also considered as the process part of the brand
Chef Yohanis products where some of chef Yohanis's on show creations are explored in collaboration with FMCG companies and made available on a larger scale. Chef Yohanis services, that includes Culinary and Hotel management consultancy.

In your opinion, what do you consider as some of the top skills needed to be a successful entrepreneur?

I believe there are numerous virtues that can be assets for anyone who wishes to be a successful entrepreneur. In my experience, I think the following are crucial for setting up a good base: Have a clear dream and set specific goals for it; Lead by example and Favour team work. Know that you don't know all and keep learning. If you are passionate enough and stubborn enough the first clue that you're on the right track will be seeing around you people who believe in what you believe.

What demographic group would you consider as your key clients?

I consider my key clients to be the global population. I believe healthy food should not be destined for a specific demographic group but rather is a basic need for all. It is the reason why I believe it is my duty and everyone's to see it given to all demographic groups.

What have been some of your challenges and lessons learned from them?

One of the main challenge I have learned from considering my clients to be the global population is being faced to a clichéd common understanding that I am trying to solve Ethiopia's' problem when in fact it is not that narrow.

It is fair to believe we now live in a global world where we are becoming closer neighbours, everyday. In that sense I also believe it is no longer enough to offer regional solutions but global ones and solving human challenges. I have learned that every culture around the world has a cultural and historical legacy (in my case being a cultural and historical culinary legacy) that can be tapped into to learn from and adapt for bettering people's lives around the globe.

In today's challenging world, what do you do to stay on top of the game?

Keep learning. When in doubt, Google it! We live in a technological world, so do not forget information is on the tip of our fingers. Then cross check because information is not necessarily knowledge.

What does success mean to you and the best way to achieve long-term success?

Considering that the same word can have different

meaning based on different perspectives and levels, for me, on a very basic level success is an emotional state of fulfilment and self-content. Again in my personal case, I will feel successful when I can make people value their heritage but also be willing to discover others in order to take the best out of every single one of them. The best way to achieve long-term success can be having a strong base, but then again I am not experienced enough to know for sure.

What has been your most satisfying moment in business?

My most satisfying moment so far has been discovering and digitizing the different culinary jewels around Ethiopia and encountering people that recognise me on the streets, and then would come to me saying thank you for making us discover who we really are.

How has being an entrepreneur affected your (family) life?

I have to be honest, my work life tends to take most of my time and though I do not have my own family yet, I am already seeing how distant I have been with my parents and siblings. It has been hard to keep track of time but I have acknowledged it as a challenge I need to solve. I have made it a priority to make time for myself and the people dear to me.

What other sacrifices have you made to be a successful entrepreneur?

It is interesting to see how above question already assumed the answer for this one☺. Some of the sacrifices I have made in the quest for success are: Friendships and enough personal time (that includes vacation, hobbies…).

On average, how many hours do you work per day and what is your typical day like?

That is actually a question I have no specific answer for. Maybe the closest truth would be I sometimes don't realise the day has ended and become night, then day again. I enjoy what I do so much, I enjoy the people I meet, and I enjoy the opportunities that come our way to the point that I am sometimes confused whether I am working or just having fun.

Where do you see yourself and business in another 10 years?

In 10 years' time I would want to be the ambassador of African cuisine globally and hope to have a brand that is recognised and trusted worldwide.

What are your guiding personal and business principles?

Having strong ethical and moral values never to cross! To earn respect by giving it. To know your worth in order to truly be hospitable and finally to value working together more than individual profit.

What is your greatest fear, and how do you manage fear?

My greatest fear is to accept failure. We all fail sometimes that is inevitable, but to accept it means to acknowledge that I am not strong enough to overcome the challenge. The way I manage fear so far is to always remind myself the reason I decided to come back to Ethiopia. Through my education and working years, I have lived abroad enough to understand that challenge is what keeps us going. Challenge is what drives discoveries, so to seek challenge means to seek answer for me. I decided to return to Ethiopia seeking challenges so I remind myself everyday that I am here to stay until my answers are revealed.

What is your best aspect of being an entrepreneur?

If this means what is my best asset as an entrepreneur, it is my passion for my work and being a decent pitcher.

Do you have role models and why?

Yes, I do. I think everyone should in order to set yourself

a height to reach and go beyond.

What are your hobbies and what do you do to relax?

I have many hobbies, though I don't practice most lately. Some of them are playing tennis, painting, paragliding, scuba-diving, dancing. Nowadays to relax, I play tennis, watch movies or grab a drink with colleagues.

Do you have any favourite quote or saying?

Yesterday is history, tomorrow a mystery but today is a gift, which is why it is called present.

What advice or message do you have for young Africans who want to become entrepreneurs?

Aim for the stars and don't let anyone tell you it's impossible. But if you aim for the stars know you have a long way to go and that every step is tougher because all eyes will be on you.

Unless you try to do something beyond what you have already mastered, you will never grow.

- Ronald Osborn, Teacher & Writer

YVETTE ATIENO ONDACHI
Ojay Greene Limited

Yvette Atieno Ondachi is the Founder of Kenya based Ojay Greene, an agribusiness entity which aggregates and purchases produce from smallholder farmers for resale in high-value urban supermarkets/restaurants. It uses a unique market driven business model to pursue its goal of "increasing the incomes of smallholder farmers in Africa."

The farmers benefit by fetching higher prices for their produce at more frequent intervals thus having a consistent income flow resulting in an improved income status.

Yvette who obtained her BSc in Bio-Chemistry from the University of Nairobi has more than 16 years of professional experience in Sales & Marketing working for top companies like AstraZeneca and GlaxoSmithKline.

The Interview:

How did the idea for your business come about?

After marketing some of the best medication (Novel discoveries in human science & research), I noticed that less that 2% of African populations could afford them. This was a painful point that made me realise I had an opportunity in using my skills to improve the livelihoods of smallholder farmers. I wanted to be a part of the solution to the high poverty levels in Africa.

Give the readers some insight into your business?

Our business is defined as a for profit social enterprise. It is a business that is entrenched in doing good for humanity, focusing on solving a social problem (high levels of societal poverty) as well as a business problem (supply gaps in a rapidly expanding market). We work with rural/peri-urban smallholder farmers to increase their incomes by linking them to knowledge, inputs & profitable urban markets. We engage the contract farming model and peer to peer learning to ensure farmers remain competitive. We incorporate the use of technology innovations to monitor outputs of farmers, standardize production and offer them real time support. This model ensures that all the players in the value chain emerge as winners, the farmer, the urban markets and Ojay Greene.

In your opinion, what do you consider as some of the top skills needed to be a successful entrepreneur?

Resilience is key. Entrepreneurship requires a will that will face the odds and choose to surmount them no matter what challenges are thrown their way.

What demographic group would you consider as your key clients?

Urban retail outlets, hotel and restaurant chains, schools, colleges, institutions and hospitals.

What have been some of your challenges and lessons learned from them?

People being human will at one time or another go back on their word; be they customers, or investors or even your team that you have entrusted with company secrets. It is critical to manage expectations and pre-decides to make things work no matter what obstacles come your way.

In today's challenging world, what do you do to stay on top of the game?

Indeed entrepreneurship can be extremely lonely; there are times all those around you think you are not thinking straight especially when things appear to go wrong. In such moments I remember the initial thing that made me leave my comfortable job to make a difference in the lives of those living below the poverty line; then I ask myself, what is the effect of giving up? It is at such moments that I remember a vow I made at the onset of this venture - failure was not an option. I draw strength from the poem that says "Rest if you must but don't quit."

What does success mean to you and the best way to achieve long-term success?

Success does not mean not making mistakes. Our education system taught us to vilify mistakes and embrace perfection. To achieve success, I realise that my greatest lessons have been from making mistakes. Therefore I embrace mistakes and use them as an opportunity to learn. This however does not mean that mediocrity is tolerated; mistakes are embraced, but repeated mistakes are discouraged. Success has to do with making one's best effort, having an open mind and a teachable attitude. This done consistently enables achieving milestones and long term success.

What has been your most satisfying moment in business?

There have been many... Satisfaction comes by validation that the sacrifice is worth it; it comes when we exceed milestones, or when our case studies are published with a global platform or when our story is told on a platform like CNN or when an old lady in the village blesses you for remembering them; All these have occurred and have brought me great satisfaction. All in all nothing comes closer to hearing of the financial growth achieved by smallholder farmers; when a farmer can take their daughter to school, or afford a nutritious meal for her dependents or afford quality healthcare for his family or even buy a new cow - these derive my most satisfying moments in the business.

How has being an entrepreneur affected your (family) life?

It has been a great sacrifice; I have had to apply myself like I've never done before. There have been many long working hours, sleepless nights, missed moments for family bonding, broken promises due to unforeseen deadlines - all this with unpredictable, little or no monetary return. I applaud my family because despite this all, they don't complain much, instead, they celebrate me as an irreplaceable member of their lives. This is one of the undeserved blessings life offers. I am thankful to God for this.

What other sacrifices have you made to be a successful entrepreneur?

Saying no to other lucrative job opportunities that have come my way; refusing to consider short term gratification and comfort for the long term reward that comes after pain and character building. I have sacrificed rest and luxuries of a balanced life. I've been exhausted nearly all year. I have promised myself that I will take a holiday soon after we have achieved some key milestones; so help me God.

On average, how many hours do you work per day and what is your typical day like?

Up to 20; a typical day is like, you have set your plans objectives and work-plan for the day, and then some curveballs are thrown your way. This is consistent with the phase we are experiencing in business - the exponential growth phase. Even with delegation, I find myself getting to my day job at 6:00 am. Just to say this doesn't happen from January to December, there are seasons when it happens; there are seasons when there is flexibility, or high level creativity but my best seasons are when my team chooses to go beyond the call of duty; I take time to celebrate them.

Where do you see yourself and business in another 10 years?

As a visionary, I see myself having developed a team of young dynamic leaders to run this venture. I see our impact reaching 1 million smallholder farmers in Africa. I see us trading around the continent, seeing food imports reduced in the continent as a direct result of our work by 2-5%. I see us as change-makers to the African agricultural landscape. I see myself championing unchartered aspects of value addition to smallholder farmers. I see us achieving sustainable development goal number. Do you want to join me on this journey?

What are your guiding personal and business principles?

Commit your plans to God and they will succeed - Proverb 16:3. Give life your best shot. It is not a rehearsal; be authentic, choose kindness, do not limit yourself. Let your dreams be outrageous. It's worth a try.

What is your greatest fear, and how do you manage fear?

The fear of breaking promises made to stakeholders - customers, smallholder farmers, team, family, cheerleaders and friends. It is an unpleasant thought and it has happened, not once but a couple of times; so what do I do? I master all the courage within me, ask God to help me and give me strength and I forge ahead, not losing sight of the big picture, encouraging myself that this phase shall pass. Together with my team, we assess our risks as frequently as once a month and ensure we have a risk mitigation plan, despite this, such opportunities have presented themselves. It is still a learning process.

What is your best aspect of being an entrepreneur?

Watching dreams become realities and even watching your expectations exceeded. When I hear about the lives changed daily, it makes the challenges worth it all.

Do you have role models and why?

Wangari Mathai. She represents an African woman of courage, influence and excellence, yet she remained humble. Her legacy to impact women still lives on through the work of her foundation.

What are your hobbies and what do you do to relax?

Spending quality time with my family is very therapeutic. I also have a group of phenomenal women whom I have walked with for close to 20 years, they are refreshing to spend time with as well. I like to read biographies of those who dared to change the world by never giving up on their dream and I draw encouragement from that.

Do you have any favourite quote or saying?

There are 2 by the late Nelson Madiba Mandela: "It always seems impossible until it's done" and "Overcoming poverty is not a gesture of charity but of justice."

What advice or message do you have for young Africans who want to become entrepreneurs?

Embrace the process, don't give up on the first sign of barriers; surround yourself with a solid group of people who will spur you on, encourage you and even chide you when the going gets tough and even when you seem to be losing your way.

Change means that what was before wasn't perfect. People want things to be better.

- Esther Dyson, Journalist

ZIBUSISO MKHWANAZI
Avatar Digital Agency

Zibusiso Mkhwanazi is the Chief Executive Officer and co-founder of Avatar, an integrated marketing agency with digital at the core.

In 2000, at the age of 17, he started his first business in Vosloosrus township, with R2 000 and a plan to create a web design company. Now, at age 33, he runs one of the fastest-growing agencies in the country.

Based in Johannesburg, South Africa, Avatar help its clients with marketing channels to make their brands desirable wherever, whenever and however people choose to engage with them. It makes this possible by uniting a professional team of marketers, creative developers, writers, strategists, account managers, producers and many others.

Avatar's clients include the world's most recognised brands such as National Geographic, Fox International Channels and South African Airways and the government of South Africa.

The Interview:

How did the idea for your business come about?

The idea of AVATAR came to me when Veli Ngubane (my current business partner) heard me speak at an event; we met and instantly became friends. It was only months later, when KrazyBoyz (my previous company at the time) was looking for Sales and Marketing director that Veli and I ended up working together. At the time Veli was part of the Strategy team at Ireland Davenport, and later became Non-Executive Director, a position he held until 2012. But he embraced the risk to leave the agency, in what seemed like a crazy decision at the time to join me in forming AVATAR - an agency that would put clients at the centre of its business paradigm and which would be committed to delivering uncommon results that truly builds businesses.

Give the readers some insight into your business?

AVATAR is a 360 agency with digital at the core. This means that we craft communication that is relevant to the consumer using today's world of mixed media including TV, social, digital, radio and so on.

We then measure results and use data to create better and more relevant communication that delivers ROI to our clients. What further distinguishes AVATAR is our diversity, which ensures that our work is relevant in different communities and reflective of South Africa's diversity.

In your opinion, what do you consider as some of the top skills needed to be a successful entrepreneur?

Dedication, faith and the ability to think independently.

What demographic group would you consider as your key clients?

Blue chip companies and the government.

What have been some of your challenges and lessons learned from them?

Learning from failure. When we don't get something right, we always find out why and how we can improve or avoid making the same mistakes.

In today's challenging world, what do you do to stay on top of the game?

I read a lot. I subscribe to feeds that keep me informed about leadership, technology and share knowledge with many people smarter than me.

What does success mean to you and the best way to achieve long-term success?

Success is fulfilling a purpose. It's when you discover a talent and each time you use it, it fulfils your existence. The best way to achieve long term success is persistence while being humble always. Don't let money change the course of why you went into business in the first place.

What has been your most satisfying moment in business?

1. Inspiring positive change to the people we work with and those that work for us.
2. Realising that our business is becoming a symbol of transformation in South Africa's advertising landscape.

How has being an entrepreneur affected your (family) life?

In order to spend more time with my family I need quality

people around me that do things better than me.

What other sacrifices have you made to be a successful entrepreneur?

I had to give up time doing cool things with my friends that all my friends did so that I could put in more effort to learn about business, technology, marketing, investments, etc. I was really hard being the odd person in a crowd but it also developed a sense of independent thinking that you don't have to do what everybody does; just do what you do really well.

On average, how many hours do you work per day and what is your typical day like?

No idea how many hours. I focus more on what has been achieved in a day. I wake up at about 3-4am and pray, gym some days, office and ministry in the evenings seven days a week.

Where do you see yourself and business in another 10 years?

I will be in full time ministry and my business will be the largest agency group in South Africa.

What are your guiding personal and business principles?

Be good to people; there are more ways of getting the best out of people than being nasty.

What is your greatest fear, and how do you manage fear?

I don't fear anything because of my faith in God.

What is your best aspect of being an entrepreneur?

The fact that you always have choices. I am able to make decisions that create a positive difference to thousands of people's lives. Love it, Love it, Love it!

Do you have role models and why?

My mom, she taught me the power of sacrifice in order to see long term gain. She raised me and my siblings as a single parent and sacrificed a better life for us to get a quality education. Her selflessness continues to inspire me to have a capitalist mind and a socialist heart.

What are your hobbies and what do you do to relax?

Honestly, on the odd month when I have a free weekend, I just lie on my couch and sleep all day.

Do you have any favourite quote or saying?

Phehelo e hlola mathata. It's a saying in Sesotho, which means perseverance defeats all troubles.

What advice or message do you have for young Africans who want to become entrepreneurs?

Always follow through with whatever you want or plan to do. It's important not just to say things, but to do them.

I learned that good judgment comes from experience and that experience grows out of mistakes.

- Omar Bradley, U.S. Army general

"Talk doesn't cook rice"

- Chinese proverb

"He who is not courageous enough to take risks will accomplish nothing in life."

- Muhammad Ali

"Twenty years from now you will be more disappointed by the things that you didn't do than by the ones you did do. So throw off the bowlines. Sail away from the safe harbour. Catch the trade winds in your sails. Explore. Dream. Discover."

- Mark Twain

ABOUT THE AUTHOR

IWA ADETUNJI read Business Management at LeTourneau University, Longview, Texas, where he graduated with B.Sc., before gaining his MBA in Telecommunications Management from the University of Dallas, Texas. He is the founder and Managing Director of Media Blackberry, the publishing company of one of Europe's foremost African oriented publications, The African Bulletin since June 2002.

KICKSTARTER

A big thank you to all our wonderful backers from our Kickstarter campaign including:

Anthony Aranse

Mr & Mrs Amadasun

Advocatenkantoor Kleijweg

THE NEXT EDITION:

Are you an African Entrepreneur or do you know one whose story is worth profiling in the next edition of *Success Stories*? Do you have related question or comment?

Send your reactions to the author @

next50ae@gmail.com

Also from MX Publishing

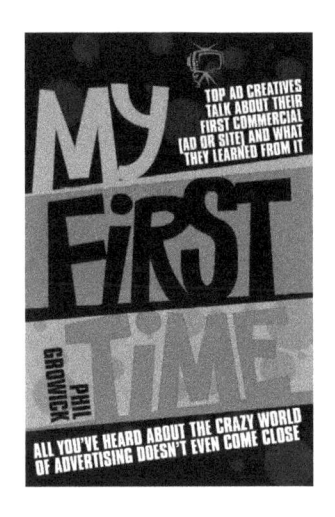

My First Time - From the top ad people all over the world, the ones who create the best TV commercials and ads, the ones you love, the ones you remember, the ones you wish you had thought of yourself, come their own stories, in their own words, about the first work they ever did. And lived to talk about it. Barely. They talk about the zaniness and craziness. They talk about the good guys and the bad girls and vice versa. They talk about things you only think can happen on TV or in the movies, but actually happened to these people. You may not believe what you will read, but in the ad world, you may not believe what you see, either. Here's a partial list (in alphabetical order) of the top global creative leaders whose stories you'll read: David Angelo (Chairman, CCO, David&Goliath) Rosie Arnold (Deputy ECD, BBH/London) Nick Bailey (ECD, AKQA/Amsterdam) David Baldwin (Lead Guitar, Baldwin &) Jamie Barrett (Partner, ECD, Goodby, Silverstein & Partners) Susan Credle (CCO, Leo Burnett) and many more.

Also from Phil Growick, *'My First Time W'* featuring the top women creatives from around the world.

Also from MX Publishing

The Secrets of Success in Brand Licensing
(English and Chinese Editions)

Brand Licensing is the most exciting and inspiring element of the marketing mix, reaching all of us in every product sector from clothing, food, giftware, household, music and publishing to stationery and toys. Brand Licenses can come from a fantastic variety of backgrounds including the arts, design, entertainment, celebrities, online and sport. Whether you are a brand owner looking to license out your brand or a manufacturer thinking of buying into a license, getting it RIGHT has never been so important. Secrets of $uccess in Brand Licensing is written by Brand Licensing Industry experts, Andrew Levy and Judy Bartkowiak who share their years of practical experience and contacts worldwide to bring you the inside story on todays successful brand licensing campaigns. What is Brand Licensing?; What makes a successful Brand License?; The process of Brand Licensing; The role of key players in Brand Licensing; Promoting your Brand License; Maximising Retail Impact; Keeping up with information and news on Brand Licensing.

Also from MX Publishing

The Happy Life Story
Saving Abandoned Children On The Streets of Nairobi

The Happy Life Story tells the brief history of an inspiring children's home project in Nairobi in Kenya. It's told through the eyes of Sharon Emecz, who after twenty years on the corporate treadmill took a career break and spent a month in Africa including volunteering at Happy Life. The main children's home is in the suburb of Kasarani. Founded in 2002, they rescue abandoned babies from the streets, many of whom are orphans. There are over 2 million orphans in Kenya and this is the heart-warming story of a small group of people saving the lives of hundreds of children. The program has expanded to a 2nd home in the village of Juja Farm where there is now also a church and a school open also to local children. Helping children get adopted is a key part of what Happy Life do with over half of the children saved being adopted. The book includes two case study interviews with adoptive parents. The book was completed when Sharon and her husband Steve return for their second Christmas at Happy Life in 2014. The book is in colour as it features many photographs. All royalties from the book go to Happy Life. You can get more information at happylifechildrenshome.com.

Lightning Source UK Ltd.
Milton Keynes UK
UKHW02f1827070818
326899UK00011B/726/P